MANAGEMENT IN EAST

Also by Vincent Edwards

Management Change in East Germany (with Peter Lawrence)
Hungary Since Communism: The Transformation of Business
  (with György Bőgel and Marian Wax)
**Transformation in the Russian Province: Enterprise Continuity
  and Change** (with Gennady Polonsky and Avgust Polonsky)
Management in Western Europe (with Peter Lawrence)

MANAGEMENT IN EASTERN EUROPE

Vincent Edwards and Peter Lawrence

palgrave

First published 2000 by
PALGRAVE
Houndmills, Basingstoke, Hampshire RG21 6XS and
175 Fifth Avenue, New York, N. Y. 10010
Companies and representatives throughout the world

PALGRAVE is the new global academic imprint of
St. Martin's Press LLC Scholarly and Reference Division and
Palgrave Publishers Ltd (formerly Macmillan Press Ltd).

ISBN 0–333–73307–X hardback
ISBN 0–333–73308–8 paperback

This book is printed on paper suitable for recycling and
made from fully managed and sustained forest sources.

A catalogue record for this book is available
from the British Library

Library of Congress Cataloging-in-Publication Data
Edwards, Vincent, 1947–
   Management in Eastern Europe / Vincent Edwards and Peter Lawrence.
      p. cm.
   Includes bibliographical references (p.) and index.
   ISBN 0–333–73307–X
   1. Management – Europe, Eastern.   2. Management – Europe, Central.
I. Lawrence, Peter A.   II. Title.

HD70.E852 E35 2000
658'.00947 – dc21   00-042055

10   9   8   7   6   5   4   3   2   1
09   08   07   06   05   04   03   02   01   00

Printed in Great Britain by
Creative Print & Design (Wales), Ebbw Uale

To
Maria and Joanne

Contents

Acknowledgements   viii

1   Management in Central and Eastern Europe: the legacy of
     the past   1
2   Hungary   15
3   Poland   31
4   Russia   43
5   Czech and Slovak management   61
6   Romania   77
7   Bulgaria   90
8   Estonia   103
9   Management in the countries of the former Yugoslavia   115
10   Past, present and future   128

Index   147

Acknowledgements

The period since 1989 has been particularly interesting and demanding for managers in Central and Eastern Europe (CEE). The research on which this book is based is largely the result of interviews with managers in the region and of visits to their companies. I am especially grateful to all those managers, from Berlin to Volgograd, who gave up their time to talk to me about their work.

I am also grateful to a number of colleagues and postgraduate students who have shared my interest in the transformation of business and management in Central and Eastern Europe. I wish to mention in particular Anne Mills, Gennady Polonsky, Frances Foster, Siobhan Bygate, Beth Kewell and Mihail-Felix Dumitrescu.

I am furthermore indebted to the many participants at the annual conferences of the Centre for Research into East European Business (CREEB) which have been organized by Buckinghamshire Business School since 1995. The conferences have brought together researchers and practitioners involved and interested in CEE from across the globe and have proved a valuable source of information, insights and contacts.

Particularly deserving of mention are those individuals who made possible the conduct of the questionnaire survey reported in Chapter 10, namely Zelimir Dulcić (University of Split), Zdenek Dytrt (Hradec Kralové), Riina Kütt (Estonian Management Institute), Győrgy Bőgel (Budapest University of Economic Sciences), Marian Gorynia (Poznan Academy of Economics), M Witek-Hajduk (Warsaw School of Economics), Gavril Budau (Transylvania University, Brasov), and Rodica Mihalea (then at Stefan cel Mare University, Suceava) and Danijel Pučko (University of Ljubljana).

I am particularly grateful for all the support, cooperation and friendship received over the years from Győrgy Bőgel and Danijel Pučko who since the early 1990s have helped to deepen my understanding of issues affecting managers in the region.

Finally, I would like to thank Jenny for the word processing and all the other support.

VINCENT EDWARDS
February 2000

Note on authorship

This book, and the companion volume *Management in Western Europe*, is our joint work. That is to say we have pooled our knowledge and ideas and in some cases engaged in jointly executed research projects. But we have divided the writing unequally between the two books, and Vincent Edwards has written all of the present work apart from the chapter on Estonia.

VINCENT EDWARDS and PETER LAWRENCE

CHAPTER 1

Management in Central and Eastern Europe: the legacy of the past

1989 was a watershed for the countries of Central and Eastern Europe (CEE) and subsequently for the countries of the former Soviet Union (FSU), as the all-embracing system of state socialism collapsed. State socialism had comprised a political system, an economic system as well as a particular form of social system: all of these elements impacted directly on the lives of individuals. In this the ruling Communist Party (whatever it actually called itself) played the leading role. This collapse of the system was not sudden, but the culmination of a process of decline and change. Although based on an ideal model of a socialist society, the system had over the years been adapted and modified to sustain its viability and promote its survival. In the end the system in CEE and the FSU succumbed to a combination of internal contradictions and external pressures. The socialist system, however, has left its legacy on the countries of the region; it could hardly have been otherwise after 75 years of communism in the Soviet Union and 45 years in the rest of CEE.

Since the former system was profoundly influential in shaping the attitudes and behaviours of individuals, it is important to appreciate the system's main characteristics and also to understand how the system operated. It is within the context of the system and its operation that the behaviour and attitudes of 'socialist' managers can be identified and understood.

The socialist system

The system consisted of a number of ideological and practical dimensions. The ideological features included the supremacy of the working class, conflict and competition with the capitalist system, the conflation of political, social and economic goals and state ownership of property.

Supremacy of the working class (or proletariat) was a basic tenet of the system. The system was portrayed as a dictatorship of the proletariat, with the ruling Communist Party as its vanguard. While the working class was glorified in theory, if not in practice, members of other classes (in particular the bourgeoisie and the aristocracy) were vilified, driven out or 'eliminated'. The centrality of the proletarian ideal, moreover, influenced views of other occupations and professions. While the working class, and especially the manual worker, was put on a pedestal, other occupations and professions were in the view of the official ideology often only second best (unless vital to the achievement of Communist Party goals). It was therefore commonplace to try to acquaint school pupils and university students with life in factories and on farms as part of their general education. Attempts to bring pupils and students into contact with 'ordinary workers' took a number of forms including regular visits to enterprises and helping out on farms at harvest time.

The socialist system, furthermore, did not separate out political, social and economic goals – these were perceived as inextricably linked. The ideal individual was a manual worker who believed in and promoted the party's policies, overachieved at work and demonstrated general concern for other individuals (at work, in society and internationally). Even though expressed here as a caricature, this ideal had enormous impact on numerous individuals who did believe in the fundamental principles of the system, even when events and reality seemed to contradict them. Socialism really did embrace powerful and attractive ideas which 'inspired' many individuals.

One of these ideas was the economic and moral superiority of socialism compared to capitalism. It has to be remembered that socialism developed in the nineteenth century as a reaction to the rise and spread of capitalism which was regarded as exploiting the majority of individuals to the benefit of a relatively small group of wealthy bourgeois. In many ways socialism sought to seize the moral high ground by claiming for itself the aim of liberating the oppressed at home and abroad. The economic imperialism of the major capitalist states was contrasted with the liberation by the forces of socialism of 'oppressed' countries from capitalist exploitation and economic oppression.

A key source of economic exploitation was identified as residing in the private ownership of property. Private ownership of property, in particular industrial assets, enabled individuals to exploit their fellows. By abolishing private property, and converting it into state property, held on behalf of society as a whole, the socialist state eliminated private property as a means of exploitation and, consequently, provided at least in theory a foundation for non-exploitative relationships in the economic and social spheres.

The socialist regimes instituted a process of nationalization of property in which in particular private owners of economic assets were expropriated. As the establishment of state property was a key policy issue of the regimes, nationalization was generally implemented rapidly so that private ownership of companies was quickly relegated to a small proportion of economic activity. In general, twenty years after the seizure of power, the socialist regimes had eliminated privately-owned companies as significant economic factors. By 1937 less than one per cent of the national income of the USSR derived from what remained of the private sector (Lavigne, 1974:17). Similarly in CEE by the end of the 1960s, the vast proportion of gross industrial and gross agricultural product and of retail trade turnover was achieved in state-owned enterprises. In this there were just two exceptions – agriculture in Poland and Yugoslavia which still remained predominantly in private hands (op. cit.:18).

These ideological principles were complemented by a number of practical aspects which permitted the principles to be turned into reality. The economy was managed through a system of centralized planning, hence the term 'command economy'. The central plan embodied the economic goals reflecting the Communist Party's economic and social aims. The central plan was extremely complex as it specified not only the broad targets of economic outputs but also the specific outputs of individual enterprises. Both the context and process of planning required inordinate quantities of data and time. The central plan as well as specifying outputs, also allocated resources to branches of industry and individual enterprises. The plan therefore also determined the allocation of inputs to production, financial resources and human resources.

The plan, moreover, was understood as a means of rationalizing the application and consumption of economic resources. The economic system was thus constrained by the volumes of inputs allocated to it by the central planners. The system was resource-constrained (Kornai, 1992). In contrast, market economies are 'demand-constrained'. That is, productive output in market economies is generally constrained only by the size of demand for particular products. It was a commonly held view within the socialist system that competition was wasteful and that resource use could be optimized by achieving economies of scale. There was therefore a tendency within the system to eliminate 'competing' products, to combine small firms into larger units and to create gigantic economic entities or industrial associations comprising numerous plants and in some instances entire branches of industry. This approach to industrial organization often resulted in the establishment of monopolies – single manufacturers and suppliers. Many of these organizations employed tens of thousands of workers.

Although the central plan was largely a national plan, there was also an element of international coordination between countries within the socialist system. This coordination took place predominantly within the framework of the Council for Mutual Economic Assistance (CMEA or COMECON) for economic issues and the Warsaw Pact for military and state security issues. Both organizations were dominated by the Soviet Union, although there is evidence that the Soviet Union actually subsidized its COMECON partners in return for political and ideological allegiance and military security (Lavigne, 1999:77).

The impact of COMECON was limited, particularly when compared with the parallel development of the Common Market/European Community in Western Europe. However, COMECON did regulate the trading relations between the CEE countries and the FSU. In addition, COMECON also instigated a degree of specialization within individual countries, creating economies of scale in certain industries such as bus production and pharmaceuticals, with the result that certain countries became a main supplier of particular products for the whole of COMECON.

Finally, the central planners set the prices of goods and services, so-called administered prices which were intended to reflect the significance and value ascribed to goods within the system. For example, essential goods such as basic foodstuffs were generally of a low price, while non-essential goods were highly priced. The mechanisms of administered prices allowed the system to ensure the widespread provision of essential goods while restricting demand for what the planners considered non-essentials. On the whole the demands of consumers enjoyed low priority, with economic policy tending to emphasize industrial goods.

The socialist enterprise

Companies (or enterprises) under the socialist system were not independent entities but were merely one component of the overall system of central planning. In line with the official ideology, enterprises had political and social as well as economic purposes and within the enterprise one could find economic, social and political functions. In addition to its economic purpose enterprises might be responsible for education and welfare, for housing and the provision of general services such as shops. Enterprises also carried out political functions and acted as bases of the ruling party.

The main economic function of the enterprise was, however, plan fulfilment. If the overall central plan was to work effectively, then individual enterprises needed to ensure that they fulfilled their own plans. In this respect, enterprises implemented the targets given to them by the central plan. As the focus of the plan was on outputs, enterprises tended to be largely production oriented. Functions such as distribution and sales, importing and exporting, and research and development, were in general handled either at the level of the industry or by separate state organizations. The main task of enterprises was to transform the raw or semi-processed materials allocated to them into the pre-determined quantity of finished products.

Within this operation costs played a secondary role as finances were balanced at the aggregate level of the central plan. Enterprises were thus subject to so-called 'soft budget constraints' (a term invented by the Hungarian economist János Kornai). Enterprises did record the costs of production. However, they were primarily responsible for fulfilling targets (one might add, irrespective of costs). Enterprises often had only a vague idea of whether they were covering their costs as they did not buy (but were allocated) raw materials and did not sell their products. Even when enterprises were subjected to financial disciplines, they could appeal to higher authorities for subsidies in order to balance their books. Political leverage could thus compensate for economic inefficiency. It was thus clearly worthwhile for managers to cultivate their political contacts rather than strive to improve the economic performance of the enterprise.

Enterprises were thus accountable not so much in financial terms but in political terms. Individual enterprises reported to the respective industrial association which in turn reported to the responsible ministry. The dominant form of relationships was therefore vertical relationships: from plan to ministry, from ministry to branch of industry and industrial association, and from there to individual enterprises. The relationships were strongly hierarchical, with, in the final analysis, the performance of individual enterprises being in theory susceptible to scrutiny by the Party's central committee.

The strong influence of political forces was also evident in the composition of the leadership (or directorate) of the enterprise. In general enterprises had a collective leadership comprising the enterprise director fulfilling an economic function, the enterprise's Party secretary and the secretary of the enterprise branch of the trade union. Decisions affecting the enterprise were in general taken collectively and reflected political and social factors as well as economic ones.

The 'socialist manager'

Many would dispute the applicability of the term 'manager' to those individuals responsible for running socialist enterprises. The main role of the socialist manager was to receive and carry out orders. Socialist managers were by and large implementers of decisions, not decision makers. Orders would be passed from level to level of the socialist hierarchy. At each level the appropriate action would be carried out and new orders passed down the line. If for any reason there was a problem, this would be referred back to the higher authority until someone was found who had the power to resolve the difficulty. There was no incentive to display individual initiative with regard to decision making. In fact this could prove counterproductive. The individual manager was thus part of a long hierarchy of officials.

Within the enterprise the manager would also be part of a collective comprising parallel Party and trades union officials. As economic aspects of the enterprise often involved social and political issues, any discussion, any incident would require the involvement of the Party and trades union.

In this regard, managers' political positions could play a significant role. The higher one was placed on the managerial hierarchy, the more likely one's political credentials would come into play. It was normal practice for managers to be party members and appointment to managerial positions, especially senior positions, was dependent more on one's political activities than on one's level of competence. This does not mean that managers by definition lacked skills and abilities but that they were in general considered secondary to political attributes. In fact, many individuals within companies were highly trained and highly skilled specialists, particularly in technical disciplines and engineering. The socialist system developed many technical specialists who subsequently occupied senior positions in enterprises. This policy went hand in hand with the fact that enterprises concentrated on production and thus required individuals who were capable of facilitating the production process.

The routine of the manager was accordingly dominated by issues relating to production. These might include obtaining the necessary inputs from designated suppliers and other sources, maintaining, repairing, upgrading and replacing plant and equipment, ensuring that the enterprise had sufficient human and financial resources, and reporting any difficulties to higher authorities.

If these issues dominated the routine, then the routine was circumscribed by the annual planning cycle and the need to meet production targets on an annual and monthly basis.

Within the workplace there was an inherent conflict between the workforce and those charged with the responsibility for ensuring that targets were achieved. It was both contradictory and somewhat ironic that the workforce, members of the working class, were directed by a group of managers and administrators who organized and saw to it that they actually carried out their tasks, managers generally working in conjunction with Party and trades union officials. Compared to managers in capitalist economies, however, socialist managers lacked many of the prerogatives available to their western counterparts. To give just one instance of this at this stage, it was virtually impossible to dismiss poorly performing or recalcitrant workers. As workers were on the whole allocated to the enterprise, managers had little say in and limited control over new employees. Even if one could have fired (and did fire) an unsatisfactory employee, there was no guarantee that his or her replacement would be any better. In fact it was generally not easy to dismiss any workers. As unemployment did not exist officially, sacking an employee was regarded as merely passing the 'problem' to another enterprise. Political and social considerations thus tended to militate against 'tough' employment policies. Such an approach clearly had a negative impact on productivity.

What, then, were the motivations and aspirations of socialist managers? In general the motivation was not monetary. Middle ranking managers might in fact earn less than skilled workers. Even enterprise directors did not earn much more than such workers. Moreover, within the socialist economy with its relative shortage of goods and services, spending the money one had was in itself a problem.

Some managers accepted managerial positions as part of the process of being allocated to an enterprise and being nominated to such a position. For some individuals it represented promotion from the shop floor, for others possibly an escape from the rigours of physical labour.

Clearly some individuals saw careers in enterprises as a means of fulfilling personal ambitions and of achieving personal aspirations for advancement and enhanced standing. As within the socialist system all positions fulfilled to a certain degree political and social functions, managerial positions within enterprises could be an element of a political career.

Furthermore, membership of an enterprise provided access to more general social resources such as housing, recreational and holiday facilities and possibly even overseas travel. Individuals in managerial positions could influence the allocation of these resources, possibly to their own advantage. The sum total of adherence to the official ideology, personal aspirations and ambitions as well as enjoyment of particular benefits could render managerial positions attractive to many individuals.

Kornai (1992: 118–121) identifies and discusses the range of factors affecting the motivation of individuals holding positions of responsibility in the social system, irrespective of their specific position, that is, whether it was in enterprises or the administration. Kornai identifies seven major influences: political and moral conviction; identification with the job; the attraction and exercise of power; prestige; material benefits; a quiet life; and finally fear of punishment. Kornai stresses that it is the overall impact of the influences which affected the behaviour of leading individuals while the impact of individual factors varied between countries and over time. The general outcome of these factors, however, is that the general characteristic of individuals in leading positions was one of 'servility and a heads-down mentality' (op. cit.:121).

If from the official viewpoint the ideal manager merely carried out orders and fulfilled the plan, the enterprise's workforce in general had a different view of what constituted the good manager. According to Adam (1996:61), 'A good manager . . . was one who was able to squeeze from the authorities an easily fulfillable plan with the allocation of sufficient inputs, including labour, and an increase in the wage bill which would guarantee an increase in the real wage without the need of much greater intensity of labour'. On balance, however, without neglecting the interests of the workforce, the socialist manager was most likely to be motivated by the factors listed by Kornai.

Even the reforms of the 1980s which expanded to a certain degree the discretion and authority of enterprise directors and managers had only limited impact, as the state bureaucracy retained overall control of economic activity.

Managers' careers continued to depend more on their relationships with their superiors than on how their enterprises performed (Kornai, 1989:48).

Disfunctions and distortions

The socialist system collapsed in part because of the disfunctions and distortions which developed and were amplified over time. Central planning and administered prices broke the relationships between supply and demand. The quantities of goods supplied and their prices were determined by the central planners; the concept of the market regulating supply and demand was banished and persisted only in peripheral areas of the economy and in practices such as bribes. Over time the prices of goods became increasingly artificial as prices for certain items were pegged for ideological reasons. The system of cross-subsidization became increasingly complex, devoid of transparency and unsustainable.

A further consequence of central planning was that the overall system was constrained by the volume of resources allocated by the planners. Resource constraints and resource misallocations resulted in inefficiencies. Stories are legion of enterprises producing shoes all of the same size and nails of a dimension which was totally impracticable for actual use in order to fulfil the production quotas. Rutland (1985:135), however, stresses that 'these tales are not merely amusing anecdotes, but identify a real and persisting fault in the soviet economy'. Allied to this was a desire to achieve the plan targets which was shared by planners, responsible people in enterprises and politicians. Deficiencies in actual economic performance were made 'good' by the manipulation of statistics and downright cheating. Rutland (1985:137), referring to Kurschnirsky, presents the example of the doubling of Soviet milk production in the period 1965–80 – a feat which could have been achieved only by watering down the milk. There are moreover possibly more innocent explanations for the distortion of official production statistics. Ryszard Kapuścinski (1994) gives an account of an irrigation project in Turkmenistan, Soviet Central Asia in the latter half of the 1960s. A brigade of Ukrainian workers is digging a branch of the canal and a female worker, Palina, records the activities of the drivers. 'And how does she keep this record? In such a way that the drivers meet their quotas . . . If a driver is nice, Palina will give him as many pencil marks as he needs to become a superquota worker' (Kapuścinski, 1994:69).

All economic resources would thus be allocated and utilized, but not necessarily in an appropriate manner. In view of the lead times required for the planning process and the general complexity of the planning system it was not surprising that what was planned did not always match requirements at the time when the plan was actually implemented as responses could be incorporated only with plan revisions or within subsequent plans.

The monopolistic nature of production, moreover, and the general absence of competition resulted in many instances in products of low quality. There was in addition limited incentive to raise the quality of products. A notable exception here was in the military sphere where competition with the Western Powers resulted in remarkable and significant developments in military and space equipment.

Finally, it proved impossible to keep the system closed from external influences. These influences were numerous and varied and included knowledge about developments and standards of living and civic behaviour in the western democracies, the impact of the Oil Shocks of the 1970s and the subsequent bouts of inflation, and the increasing technological gap between the competing systems in many spheres. For example, the return on exports from the socialist system diminished rapidly as their attractiveness declined in comparison to western products, with the result that it was costing the socialist countries more and more resources to obtain the same amount of foreign currency.

Enterprises too had to respond to the deficiencies in the implementation of the system. One manifestation of this was the quest by enterprises for autarky (self-sufficiency). As the enterprise could not rely on receiving the resources allocated to it or on receiving them on time, enterprises developed measures to circumvent these deficiencies. Enterprises would build up reserves of raw materials and personnel in an attempt to be able to resolve their difficulties out of their own resources. Enterprises would also develop unofficial relationships with suppliers and other organizations so that they could obtain the materials and services they needed if the system let them down. In order to achieve the plan, the plan was often circumvented. Not surprisingly, in addition to production, purchasing departments played a key role in socialist enterprises as they could remedy, often by means of informal agreements, at least in part the deficiencies of the planning system.

A further distortion was in the nature of the routine within socialist enterprises. Failures in the supply of material inputs and break-downs of often aged machinery resulted in frequent periods of zero production. In order to meet monthly and annual targets, there would be a period of frenetic activity at the end of each month/year when even office workers would be drafted in to the production process. These regular periods of so-called 'storming' also became part of the enterprise routine.

As mentioned earlier, managers did not make decisions, they followed orders, and they were rewarded and promoted accordingly. Plan fulfilment was paramount and might require collective action to remedy the deficiencies of the system. However, personal initiative was in general neither encouraged nor likely to be appreciated – it might be viewed as arrogance or, even worse, knowing better than one's superiors and the Party. In general therefore the system required managers to be passive rather than active and proactive. This attitude reflected a system which on the whole developed only slowly and in the end too slowly for it to survive.

Everyday life under socialism

Life under socialism was not renowned for its excitement and vivacity. The general conditions of life – from food to housing – were generally adequate but drab. The vast majority of the population had to endure the same conditions. Only the party elite enjoyed access to a higher standard of living.

Individual pursuits were, moreover, discouraged and regarded with suspicion. The ideal was collective activity even in the recreational sphere – holidays at enterprise or trades union holiday camps, company visits to the theatre, etc. Frequently housing conditions (small, low-quality flats; shared housing) made any privacy virtually unobtainable.

People tended to work long hours; long hours were also spent looking and queuing for food and other items to purchase. 'Luxury' items such as cars could be obtained only after waits of years and years.

Not surprisingly, people sought to create their own private spheres (for example, by building and cultivating second homes, so-called *datschas*) and to circumvent the shortages inherent in the system. Pilfering from the workplace was endemic. Bribery in various forms was not uncommon. Regular little gifts to a shop assistant could ensure acquisition of a new pair of shoes when stocks actually arrived. Such practices, however, were no more than a limited response to 'a system that was continuously unable to provide for its citizens' needs for forty years or more' (Drakulic, 1993:189).

System change

Towards the end of 1989 the socialist system was subjected to a series of shocks, encapsulated dramatically by the opening of the Berlin Wall. One after the other the socialist regimes gave in or were driven out. 1991 witnessed the end of the socialist system in the Soviet Union and the demise of the Soviet Union itself.

Even if in reality the system change did not occur overnight, conceptually there was only one viable alternative to socialism, namely capitalism and the market economy. The system change can be analysed at a number of levels and numerous authors have categorized the implications of the system change in terms of managerial thinking and behaviour (Edwards and Foster, 1994).

At the level of the overall economy, central planning disappeared – this did not mean the disappearance of governmental direction or influence though the manner in which they operated generally changed. However, central planning as a means of allocating resources and determining volumes of outputs ceased to be practised. The new concepts in the economies of CEE were now marketization, that is, the establishment of market economies, privatization, the transfer or retransfer of state-owned property into private ownership, and competition. In line with these concepts came market-based pricing, the application of the laws of supply and demand in product and labour markets and the opening of domestic markets to foreign competitors.

The system change was enthusiastically received by the majority of the inhabitants of Central and Eastern Europe. This enthusiasm was grounded in a rejection of the experience of socialism with its limited freedoms and endemic shortages and a desire to attain the standard and style of life perceived to be typical of the advanced western economies. The system change engendered a high level of aspiration, in short, that life would become better. Such a view was in part fuelled by western opinion shapers and commentators. Such aspirations, however, have not proved so easy to fulfil.

At the level of the firm the system change also had enormous implications. From being formerly largely production units, enterprises were now extricated from the constraints of central planning and became independent decision-making entities. Organizations which had been used to accepting orders from higher authorities now had to identify and carve out an independent existence. What and how much to produce was now up to the company itself as were other decisions relating to business scope, strategy and survival. Such decisions often had to be taken at the same time as the company was undergoing the privatization process, which on occasions actually involved the company itself looking out for new owners. It was generally hoped that new owners would bring expertise and much needed funding.

Above all the system change meant that companies had now to operate within a different set of rules, that is, those of the market economy; companies had to follow these rules often in competition with far more experienced players. Not surprisingly many formerly state-owned companies felt themselves subjected to enormous pressures. These pressures forced the pace of company transformation. Companies reviewed the range of goods they offered (as well as their quality); they compared them with those of the competition. Often this resulted in a narrower, more focused portfolio of products. Companies also reviewed the range of activities in which they had been involved. It became commonplace for companies to give up their social activities such as housing and medical provision. This was frequently carried out with a heavy heart, but such activities were generally regarded as a burden on companies and the sale of facilities such as holiday homes and educational and medical centres (as well as of surplus land and buildings) generated new resources for more fundamental aspects of company restructuring.

The system change overturned the traditional departmental hierarchies within organizations. As the socialist economies had been resource-constrained and target-driven, the primary role had been taken by purchasing and production departments – that is, by those departments which obtained the inputs and those which created the finished products. These departments now declined in importance as the pressure was now on the marketing and sale of products – functions which previously had in general been outside of the control of the enterprises themselves and had been exercised by centralized state organizations. This switch from a purchasing-cum-production orientation to one based on marketing and sales was a tremendous challenge to companies as the intellectual resources and capabilities required for such a fundamental change in orientation were neither easy to obtain nor develop, at least in the short term.

In consequence managers were expected to demonstrate new attitudes and behaviours: in sharp contrast to the recent past they had to display initiative and independent thinking and decision-making. Creativity and innovation were now desired characteristics. The pedestrian security of the past had to give way to risk-taking, tolerance of ambiguity, opportunity seeking and individualism. Many managers were unable to rise to such a challenge: some went into retirement; others tried to continue in the same old way. Some managers adapted very quickly to the system change: almost overnight they changed from communist cadres to capitalist managers (in some cases owners), earning the sobriquet of 'wrynecks' or turncoats as well as a certain envy and contempt from people at large. Many managers, however, rose to the challenge of the new circumstances: many of these managers had felt held back by the former system, in many instances because they were not Communist Party members. The change of system gave them the opportunity to rise within the company hierarchy and assume positions of significant responsibility. Allied to the desire for personal advancement – a desire to practise real management – many managers were motivated by a desire to help their colleagues and their local communities by ensuring the survival and transformation of the enterprise.

The system could not but have an enormous impact on everyday life. The one-party state was replaced by democratic political structures in a variety of guises. The oppressiveness of the former regimes evaporated in most countries in the region.

However, the security of the world of work also vanished. Unemployment and competition became realities, often harsh realities. The shortage of goods disappeared, to be replaced for many by a shortage of money. New freedoms (for example, to travel abroad) could not always be afforded. Without doubt everyday life changed substantially, but whereas previously the uniformity of socialism had been spread within society more or less uniformly, the new system was betokened by widening social disparities in income levels and in wealth.

The impact of the former system, moreover, could not be swept away overnight, even if external appearances changed. More than 40 years of socialism in Central and Eastern Europe and more than 75 years of the system in Russia and the former Soviet Union did not disappear without trace. 'The reality is that communism persists in the way people behave, in the looks on their faces, in the way they think' (Drakulic, 1993: xxiv).

Homogeneity and diversity

We have so far discussed the socialist system as if it were a homogeneous entity. From a number of perspectives the constituent republics of the Soviet Union and the countries of CEE were highly diverse, and this diversity is significant in understanding how the system took shape in the individual countries and how managerial behaviour differed and differs. Leaving the Soviet Union to one side, the countries of CEE which adopted the socialist system after 1945 were diverse in a number of ways. Most of the countries were predominantly agricultural before 1945, although they contained pockets of industrialization. Industrialization was thus generally accelerated by the socialist regimes. The exceptions to this generalization were the Czech part of Czechoslovakia and East Germany which had been in the forefront of continental European industrialization in the nineteenth century. These two areas therefore already possessed a strong industrial culture and a tradition of industrial management.

In addition, there were differences in the way in which a socialist economic system was implemented. This affected the nature and pace of privatization and industrial restructuring. We have already noted that agriculture in Poland and Yugoslavia tended to remain in private ownership. Yugoslavia, moreover, after its break with the Soviet Union in 1948, developed its own distinctive economic system which we will examine in Chapter 9. The history of the region since 1945 indicates the difficulties experienced by the regimes in implementing their policies and in gaining general support for the socialist ideal. This was often compounded by the failure of the system to deliver what the population wanted. Some countries (East Germany, Czechoslovakia after the defeat of the Prague Spring in 1968 and Bulgaria) followed most closely the Soviet model of economic management. For much of the postwar period East Germany (the German Democratic Republic) was regarded as the showpiece of the Soviet economic system in Europe.

Other countries, however, were less rigorous (or more inventive) in their development of a socialist economic system. Relatively more private economic activity was allowed to operate (as in the case of Polish agriculture) or more attention was given to satisfying the demands of the population as in the case of Hungary after the defeat of the 1956 uprising. We will return to 'goulash' communism in the next chapter. At the other extreme the Ceausescu regime in

Romania pursued a harsh economic policy at home in order to eliminate the country's foreign debt.

Within the parameters of the Soviet model, therefore, events and decisions at the national level tended to differentiate the ways in which the system was implemented and operated in individual countries. This diversity was also a feature of the Soviet Union which covered a large area of the globe and encompassed many nationalities and regions with wide discrepancies in the level of economic development. As long as the Soviet Union was able to exert its control over the countries of CEE, the general characteristics of the Soviet model were evident and the national differences remained of only secondary importance. The period since 1989, however, has witnessed the disappearance of the Soviet model from CEE and the FSU as well as a resurgence of national identities.

References

Adam, J. (1996) *Why did the Socialist System Collapse in Central and Eastern European Countries? The case of Poland, the former Czechoslavakia and Hungary*, Basingstoke and London: Macmillan.

Drakulic, S. (1993) *How We Survived Communism And Even Laughed,* London: Vintage.

Edwards, V. and Foster, F. (1994) 'Meeting the Need for Management Development in Eastern Europe', *The International Journal of Educational Management*, 8, 1, pp. 14–19.

Kapuścinski, R. (1994) *Imperium*, London: Granta Books.

Kornai, J. (1989) 'The Hungarian Reform Process: Visions, Hopes and Reality' in Nee, V. and Stark, D. (eds) *Remaking the Economic Institutions of Socialism: China and Eastern Europe*, Stanford: Stanford University Press, pp. 32–94.

Kornai, J. (1992) *The Socialist System, the Political Economy of Communism*, Princeton: Princeton University Press.

Lavigne, M. (1974) *The Socialist Economies of the Soviet Union and Europe*, London: Martin Robertson.

Lavigne, M. (1999) *The Economics of Transition, from Socialist Economy to Market Economy*, Basingstoke and London: Macmillan, 2nd ed.

Rutland, P. (1985) *The Myth of the Plan, Lessons of Soviet Planning Experience*, London: Hutchinson.

CHAPTER 2

Hungary

Hungary has been one of the success stories of the post-communist transformation in Central and Eastern Europe. Politically, Hungary has been in the forefront of establishing a democratic system. Already towards the end of the former regime there were strong signs of political liberalization and it was the Hungarian authorities that, by opening Hungary's borders with Austria in the middle of 1989, created the breach in the Iron Curtain which permitted many individuals to flee to Western Europe. This decision by the Hungarian authorities was a clear milestone in the final collapse of the communist regimes of the region. Since 1989 Hungary has established a working democracy reflecting a broad range of political views, including former communists, and has witnessed an alternation of governments, led on one occasion by the former, albeit reformed, communists themselves.

Economically too, Hungary has enjoyed considerable success and is one of the first wave of former communist countries being considered for membership of the European Union. By 1998 the private sector was generating 80 per cent of gross domestic product (GDP) and employing 75 per cent of the workforce. This was a notable economic transformation as in 1984 the state sector in Hungary had produced 65 per cent of value added, compared to just over 10 per cent in the UK and only one per cent in the USA (Lawrence, 1998:84). Furthermore, external trade had been substantially reorientated from CEE and the FSU to western markets, with the EU accounting, in 1998, for 73 per cent of Hungarian exports and 64 per cent of imports (*Wirtschaftslage und Reformprozesse in Mittel- und Osteuropa*, 1999:7–10). Hungary moreover had received the lion's share of foreign direct investment (FDI) entering CEE and the Baltic states. Over the period 1989–97 Hungary received 36 per cent of the total FDI in this region (EBRD, 1998:17). All in all – in spite of persisting difficulties in areas such as employment – Hungarians enjoy one of the highest standards of living, as measured by per capita GDP, in the region.

The current achievements of the Hungarian economy are built in part on certain aspects of the former system of economic management, in particular the relatively pragmatic approach to management of the economy and enterprises and the entrepreneurial aspirations of the Hungarians themselves. Hungary is also an interesting example of the diversity existing behind the monolithic facade of the Soviet model.

Hungary under communism

The Red Army occupied Hungary in 1944. From the end of the Second World War in 1945 onwards therefore the organization of the economy and of society in general was modelled closely on the ideological principles and practices of the Soviet Union. The actual implementation of the Soviet model in Hungary went through a number of distinct stages (Csapó, 1975; Pető, 1990).

The first stage, from 1945 to 1948, has been described as a transitional stage. It was the period in which Hungary had to try to come to terms with the devastation of the Second World War and become resigned to its position within the Soviet sphere of influence – in other words it was the period in which the Hungarian Communist Party took over all the levers of power.

The second stage covered the years from 1948 to 1968 in which the 'classical' or 'directive' model of economic management was implemented. Problems with implementation in the Hungarian setting quickly became manifest and some minor corrections were introduced from 1953. However, economic decisions had to play second fiddle to political concerns, especially after the massive popular uprising against communist rule in 1956. Further small reforms were undertaken from 1964 but by then there was a growing awareness of a need for radical change.

The third stage covers the years from 1968, the period of the so called 'guided market model' or 'new economic mechanism'. In this period there was an attempt to implement the concept of market socialism, although there was already a certain retrenchment in the late 1960s and early 1970s.

Hungary in 1945 was still a predominantly agrarian economy, with 50 per cent of the labour force employed in agriculture. The common programme of 1944, agreed by a coalition of parties (including the Communists) in areas of eastern Hungary liberated by the Soviet army, professed a continuing commitment to a market economy. In fact this declaration had been followed by a widespread land reform which expanded substantially the number of families that owned land by redistributing land previously owned by large landowners. However, from 1945 there was increasing evidence of a drive to limit the operations of the market and set up a system of centralized economic management. This drive was pursued consistently by the Communist Party. Firstly there was the nationalization of certain key activities such as coal mining and of foreign trade. German-owned assets were taken over by the Soviet authorities and formed the basis for the establishment of Hungarian-Soviet mixed enterprises.

Secondly, as a consequence of the desperate economic situation and the need to continue managing the economy almost on a war basis, at the end of 1945 an enabling act was passed which gave the government powers to act by decree. Economic decision making passed into the hands of the Supreme Economic Council (SEC) which was controlled by the Communists. The SEC actively sought to restrict the operation of the market and reduce the proportion of private property.

The economic situation in Hungary in 1945 was truly desperate. The money and capital markets had collapsed and payment was frequently in kind and barter. In order to maintain economic activity material management bureaus were re-established by the government to collect and distribute raw and primary materials. The collapse of money markets enabled the SEC to play the key role in allocating credit to companies. As a result of the SEC's credit allocation policies the majority of private companies became insolvent and were subsequently nationalized.

Further measures to constrain the market included the fixing of prices for agricultural products independently of world market prices in 1946 and the nationalization of the banking system in 1947. In 1948 companies employing more than 100 employees were also nationalized. This measure brought the majority of industrial activity under state control. Even though agriculture was still largely in private hands, it had nonetheless been brought into the overall system of centrally controlled economic management.

The 'directive' model of economic management

In April 1949 Hungary formally adopted a Soviet-style constitution. The implementation of the Soviet 'directive' model of economic management also got under way. Csapó (1975:63) outlines six main principles for the implementation of the 'directive' model in Hungary. First, industrialization had to be promoted to create a modern economy. Second, agriculture was to be 'industrialized' through collectivization. A further aim was to eliminate private ownership in this sector. Third, education and training were to be expanded to meet the requirements of the aforementioned economic goals (although this was also promoted for ideological reasons). Fourth, self-sufficiency (autarky) of economic sectors was to be achieved particularly with regard to steel and machinery. Fifth, the purpose of foreign trade was closely circumscribed and focused on facilitating the import of raw materials and equipment. Sixth, centralized planning was introduced.

Enterprises, moreover, became formal parts of the state administration and enterprise managers were appointed according to political criteria (e.g. political reliability and party membership). The enterprise thus became integrated in a hierarchical state system of industrial ministries and functional bodies such as local government organizations.

Concurrent with these developments, was a change in industrial organization and structure as specialization increased. This took a number of forms. Enterprises became predominantly production units and activities such as sales and marketing were detached from the control of independent enterprises and coordinated centrally. The impetus to pursue and achieve specialization on the part of enterprises came from a belief that (a) competition was wasteful and unnecessary and (b) economies of scale could be attained by creating units concentrating on limited ranges of activity on a national scale. The chief tool of economic management, however, was the plan.

A number of factors mitigated against the successful implementation of the centralized planning system. These included difficulties of data collection and processing as well as the sheer complexity of the interrelationships within the system (Kornai, 1990). The dual system of party and state controls also tended to create confusion rather than clarity in an already highly complex situation.

A further factor hampering the implementation of the 'directive' model was Hungary's relative smallness compared to the Soviet Union. Specialization and a striving for economies of scale resulted in the establishment of monopolistic enterprises. A small country such as Hungary was more dependent on foreign trade and could not strive to be self-sufficient in the same way that a large country like the Soviet Union could. With the foundation of COMECON in 1949 Hungary's foreign trade relations became increasingly oriented to its COMECON partners, in particular the Soviet Union. By 1960 over 60 per cent of Hungary's foreign trade was with its COMECON partners. Specialization within COMECON was encouraged and Hungary became a major manufacturer of buses (Ikarus), pharmaceuticals and at a later date consumer electronics. This specialization was, however, dependent on the overall requirements of the members of COMECON.

The Hungarian uprising

The popular uprising against the communist regime in 1956 proved a significant watershed in Hungarian politics and had a direct impact on the implementation of the Soviet model. The regime was clearly shaken by the scale of popular dissatisfaction and János Kádár's rule was typified by a policy of 'doing the same better' rather than 'doing something different'. Kádár remained in power from November 1956 to the middle of 1988. His period in office was characterized by a stress on continuity, gradualism and a recognized need to fulfil the population's material needs. Kádár's approach has been frequently described as goulash communism. Society became increasingly depoliticized and in the 1960s a 'second' economy based on non-state income was permitted to expand and contribute to rising living standards. These developments, however, failed to mask the weaknesses of the economic system.

In the period 1962–64 there was a further reorganization of enterprise structure which resulted in an increase in the number of enterprises employing over 1000 employees and a corresponding decline in the number of those employing less than 1000. The number of enterprises employing over 1000 employees rose from 197 in 1960 to 254 in 1965. There were 10 enterprises in 1965 with over 10 000 employees (Pető, 1990:40). This reorganization did not lead to the expected improvements in performance and did no more than create large organizations which developed priorities of their own, militating against the aims and purposes of the central plan.

The twin policies of collectivization and industrialization had transformed the structure of the Hungarian economy. Agricultural employment dropped from 50 per cent to 39 per cent of employment between 1945 and 1960. Industry, however, still employed only 28 per cent of the total workforce in 1960. By 1970 this position had been reversed, with industry employing 37 per cent and agriculture only 26 per cent of the total workforce (Pető, 1990:39).

The 'guided market' model

The second Five Year Plan of 1956–60 and its reformulation for the period 1961–65 were disappointing and failed to ensure the achievement of the respective plans' goals. With the growing realization of these failures there was increasing discussion of the need to overhaul the system and to introduce new economic mechanisms.

It was argued that the linkage between the macro plan and micro plans needed to be mediated through a range of economic mechanisms (e.g. economic regulatory instruments). Micro plans were to be implemented within the context of a market which was regulated by economic mechanisms so as to ensure compliance with the general aims of the macro plan. In contrast to the 'directive' model, this approach was described as a 'guided market' model (Csapó, 1975).

The debate about economic models was subject to both economic and political considerations, relating to the official ideology, the political situation in Hungary and practice throughout COMECON. Many Hungarian communists objected to the concept of the market, even if guided by the state and the Communist Party. However, from 1965 there was increasing mention of the new economic mechanisms.

How did the 'guided market' model differ from the 'directive' model? First, the macro plan ceased to be compulsory for individual enterprises which were no longer subject to mandatory targets. Targets became increasingly flexible and alternative plans were also developed. 'The underlying principle of the reform was a combination of planned economy with the advantages of the market ...' (Pető, 1990:45). On the whole this was viewed by the government as basically a technocratic response to the failures of the 'directive' approach rather than as the replacement of the Soviet model.

The substitution of indirect economic mechanisms for plan instructions was a distinctive feature of the Hungarian system of economic management and was not imitated to any substantial degree in any other of the COMECON countries. The so-called reforms, however, did not change the fundamental nature of the system but redistributed power from the central state organizations and the ministries to the bodies responsible for implementing the new economic mechanisms, for example, the Central Bank.

Enterprise autonomy, moreover, while enlarged in theory, remained largely circumscribed, especially for the large state enterprises; for example enterprises had only limited discretion to amend wage levels (and certainly no discretion to reduce wages). Although various categories of prices were introduced – i.e. administered, limited and free prices – in practice price controls continued to operate. On the whole, the autonomy, flexibility and decentralization promised by the 'guided market' model were considerably constrained. Moreover, improvements in performance were short-lived. It was clearly difficult for enterprises to make use in practice of their autonomy when they were locked into agreements with partners in COMECON and also with Western companies (Barratt Brown, 1984:142).

The 1970s and 1980s

In spite of the 'market mechanisms' of the 'guided market' model the objective conditions of Hungary's situation within COMECON allowed enterprises only a limited space for manoeuvre. 'Guidance' predominated over any semblance of the market. The Hungarian reforms, moreover, were regarded as ideologically suspect by its COMECON partners, especially in the aftermath of the crushing of the Prague Spring in 1968.

The Oil Shock of 1973 also worked against the development of the 'guided market' model as the government reined in the strands of autonomy enjoyed by companies. However, this retrenchment was also accompanied by a continuing desire on the part of the government to satisfy the material needs of the population. This involved permitting the existence of private enterprise, even if only on a limited scale. A further feature was the increase of economic links with the West, which took the form of hard currency loans and joint ventures, although the government believed it could hold back the effects of the Oil Shock and other effects of world market forces at Hungary's western border. These developments, however, only served to accentuate the contradictions of the Hungarian economic situation which continued to deteriorate and ultimately contributed to the fall of Kádár in 1988 and the subsequent collapse of the communist regime.

At least in theory the 'market-guided' system removed the overt relationship between the central plan and the activities of individual enterprises. Compared to the classical model greater weight was given to horizontal (i.e. market) relationships. Plan targets still existed but were no longer binding. Enterprises were encouraged to pay greater attention to consumer demands, to become entrepreneurial, to seek profits and greater efficiency. According to Bőgel and Huszty (1999) some Hungarian enterprises undertook corporate strategic thinking from the late 1970s. In the 1980s, moreover, some enterprises adopted non-functional organizational forms such as matrix and divisional structures (Dobák and Tari, 1996). All in all, however, the New Economic Mechanism was still anchored within the prevailing ideology and the existing institutions of the communist state.

The New Economic Mechanism was intended to promote the responsiveness and efficiency of enterprises, not to create a market economy or to undermine the foundation of the existing social and political system. At best it was intended to reconcile the potentially conflicting interests of the party on the one hand and the rest of society on the other.

Nevertheless it would be extreme to dismiss the impact of the economic reforms on enterprises. From being purely a component of an integrated system enterprises did acquire some autonomy. This impacted immediately on those directing the enterprises now that they were permitted some freedom of action outside the limits of the plan. When measured against the freedom of action enjoyed by senior managers in companies in western market economies, this increase in enterprise discretion appears severely limited. However, when contrasted with the other countries of the region, Hungary was in the forefront of adopting a more market-oriented approach to its economic system (Samli and Jermakowicz, 1983). Out of the communist regimes of central and eastern Europe only Yugoslavia was regarded as being more open to market forces.

This naturally leads us on to the question of how, on what basis one became a 'manager' (or enterprise director) under the communist system. Throughout the life-span of the former regime there was a tension between professional competence and political acceptability. Clearly, the regime would not appoint individuals to senior positions who were inimical or even only luke-warm to the regime. On the other hand there was a recognition of the need for certain skills and competencies in managing economic organizations. As a generalization over the period of communist rule the stress on political acceptability was mitigated in favour of professional competence.

In the late 1940s, with the take-over of power, the regime was concerned to ensure that the newly nationalized enterprises as well as other economic institutions (such as the banks) were directed and managed by individuals who were committed to the official ideology and to establishing a command economy. On account of this, party membership (or at least support for the aims of the regime) were important criteria for the appointment of individuals to leadership positions. After 1956, with the decision to try to satisfy the material needs of the population, and with the subsequent decentralization introduced by the New Economic Mechanism, non-party specialists were also employed. By the 1970s professional competence had gained in importance. However, professional competence in itself was insufficient for the more senior positions in enterprise management. While professional competence was sufficient for those wishing to become middle managers, party political affiliations were essential if one aspired to top management positions.

These requisite party affiliations could be gained through membership of the Communist Party or related organizations such as the Youth League. Passive membership would in itself be deemed insufficient and anyone wishing to be considered for a senior managerial position would need to have played an active role in party political or related activities.

A number of other factors played an important role in the career paths of managers. In the early days of the regime working class origins were considered important and many managers had working class backgrounds. This fitted in well with the official ideology. On the whole, however, educational qualifications were also of significance. This bias towards class origins re-emerged in the retrenchment of the early 1970s when the regime reined in some of the concessions associated with the New Economic Mechanism (Falus Szikra, 1995:79). Attempts to facilitate the development of young workers for managerial positions were on the whole unsuccessful (ibid.). Nevertheless, numerous managers were graduates of the evening Marxist-Leninist University. Although their qualifications were popularly disparaged as Foxi-Maxi diplomas after a well-known cartoon character, they were highly regarded by the political establishment. With this pressure on educational development one might have expected the younger generation of managers to be better qualified than their older counterparts. However, this was in fact not the case (op.cit.:86).

By the 1980s the situation had further changed. The declining significance attached to political allegiances had not in fact been counterbalanced by a greater emphasis on professional competence. Political allegiance in a general sense had yielded in pre-eminence to the exploitation of personal contacts and patronage. By the mid-1980s, according to Babus and Mézes (1985), quoted in Falus Szikra (1995:81): 'In Hungary the dominant factors determining advance (*sic*) and self-assertion were personal relations. Public and political activities were ranked second, leadership ability third. These were followed by servility, knowledge, pushing, the support by the collective, seniority and chance'. A favoured route into top management positions comprised university study, followed by an official position in the party's youth organization. This enabled the individual to gain organizational experience and more importantly to make personal contacts to be drawn on when it was time to leave the youth organization (normally when one had reached one's late twenties). After such an experience and with the support of the right contacts one could be appointed to a senior position (e.g. CEO or deputy CEO, even of a large company).

The relative decentralization of economic management introduced with the New Economic Mechanism undoubtedly increased the area of at least top management discretion. So much so, in fact, that already at the beginning of the 1970s there was widespread criticism of managerialism and some concessions in the direction of greater enterprise autonomy were retracted. Nevertheless, there was increased discretion and it manifested itself in a number of ways, particularly with regard to labour, i.e. the number of people employed and their overall remuneration (Swain, 1992:162). By western standards the extent of the increase may appear small and in many respects inconsequential. Compared with the situation in the other countries of the Soviet bloc, however, the Hungarian reforms appeared substantial and to some observers a dangerous development.

It is well known that the command economies had a far narrower spread of wages and salaries in comparison to western market economies. Incomes were, on average, both lower and less variable. These factors can be largely attributed to ideological reasons, namely that the state provided extensive social services and that it would be ideologically unsound for the incomes of non-workers to exceed excessively those of the working class. Compared to their counterparts in Bulgaria, Czechoslovakia, Poland and the German Democratic Republic, Hungarian senior managers were regarded as receiving conspicuously high salaries (not including other benefits and perquisites). For example, in the 1970s the salaries of senior managers was approximately twice the national average wage, while those of middle managers was about one third above the national average. Such wage differentials were particularly conspicuous in a society avowedly based on egalitarianism and the central role of the working class. Such disparities were moreover not limited to a small section of the working population as the number of white-collar positions within companies had mushroomed since 1949 and it was not unusual for a medium-sized company to have six or seven managerial levels (Falus Szikra, 1995:88–9).

Top managers in particular were often regarded as a race apart. They were popularly and jocularly characterized by reference to five objects which were considered as the status symbols of the socialist (!) manager in the old regime. In Hungarian these were known as the five K's: car (*kocsi*), own house or flat (*kégli*), dog (*kutya*), government telephone line (*k-vonal*) and mistress (*kurva*). Senior management positions were therefore seen as opportunities to acquire benefits and wealth beyond the reach of normal workers, hence the widespread resentment of what was regarded as excessive privilege.

A key area of management discretion was the allocation of bonuses. A substantial proportion of individual incomes consisted of an element of bonus. This could constitute as much as 200 per cent of the basic wage (Pearce, 1993:119). Bonuses were generally allocated by one's immediate superior. Although one of the criteria for the allocation of the bonus was performance, bonuses were largely awarded as a result of personal connections. The allocation of bonuses tended to resemble an inverted pyramid with the majority of enterprise funds ear-marked for bonuses being awarded to senior managers. For example, the system of distribution of the profit-sharing fund to enterprise members in the late 1960s attracted considerable criticism when it emerged that senior executives could receive 'dividends' equivalent to up to 80 per cent of their salaries while the majority of employees were restricted to a maximum of 15 per cent of their wages. There was widespread condemnation of this approach and it was modified in 1970 (Csapó, 1975:122–5). The inclusion of bonuses and other perquisites (legal and illegal) in the calculation of incomes would certainly have widened the officially presented gap in incomes between top managers and the rest of the population even further. Not surprisingly top managers were one of the wealthiest groups in Hungarian society.

It is worth reiterating that the discretion of senior managers within Hungarian enterprises was by western standards still severely circumscribed. In the first instance the overall framework of economic management gave managers limited scope for individual initiative. This was further hampered by a range of government regulations which precluded initiatives at enterprise level, e.g. in the area of wage negotiations. Balaton (1998:36), referring to Dobák, describes the situation of Hungarian managers in the 1980s in the following way:

> During the 80s both market requirements and expectations of state hierarchy have influenced the behaviour of managers in Hungary. To meet the requirements of hierarchy, external driven role perception was necessary. At the same time adaptation to the market required internal driven managerial role perception. To meet the two kinds of requirements made many executives confused. That is the reason that Hungarian managers were described as 'Janus-faced' in the period before the socio-political changes.

The corollary of this limited discretion was that there was also less scope for individual mistakes. Even when errors did occur which necessitated the removal of a senior manager the response was normally 'forgiving' in that the senior manager would be 'kicked upstairs' to a 'safe' position such as advisor to one of the ministries, member of an enterprise board or director of personnel!

All in all, until the very end of the regime, the criterion of professional competence played at best a subsidiary role in the appointment of top managers. This had a number of reasons. Firstly, managers in part tended not to be replaced. So, for example, the senior managers appointed in the early post-war period were not replaced as a consequence of the shift of emphasis of the New

Economic Mechanism, in spite of the professed greater stress on professional competence. Second, allegiance to the ruling party yielded to the exploitation (and abuse) of personal contacts.

In general, managers were not replaced as a result of changes in economic policy. As many managers appointed in the early post-war period were relatively young, they remained in office even when the system of economic management shifted in emphasis from central planning to greater decentralization.

This is not to say that all managers lacked or failed to display any of the characteristics of successful managers in the west. In fact Ehrlich and Révész (1995:17) note the many positive developments which had taken place in Hungarian agriculture, largely because of the entrepreneurism of the managers working in this sector, as well as other positive factors in pharmaceuticals and applied physics.

In the context of the COMECON countries, according to Witold Kiezun (1991) Hungarian managers tended to have a less autocratic management style than many of their COMECON counterparts, Polish managers excepted. They were also more likely to voice their criticisms. On the other hand, the motivation of Hungarian managers was lower than that of managers in East Germany or Czechoslovakia. This lower degree of motivation seemed to go hand in hand with lower productivity. The relations between management and workers in Hungary (and Poland) were also more strained than elsewhere in COMECON, for in Hungary workers were liable to undertake individual and private initiatives to counterbalance the constraints imposed by management in the enterprise.

It would be wrong, however, to regard the introduction of the 'guided market' model as a complete failure. In comparison to many of the other countries of central and eastern Europe which had remained more closely aligned to the Soviet model many features such as enterprise autonomy and non-administered prices, both conceptually and practically, provided Hungary with a sounder preparation for its transition to a market economy.

Managers and the transition to a market economy

In spite of the benefits accruing to Hungarian managers from the more liberal economic regime as embodied in the 'guided market' model, research undertaken on Hungarian managers in the early 1990s (Edwards and Foster, 1994) indicated that attitudes and behaviours which had become established under the former system were still widespread. These aspects were manifested in non-entrepreneurial perspectives and practices. To give just one example of this, a producer of cast iron bathtubs commented:

At present the main objective of restructuring is to establish an organisation that works steadily and safely and which is capable of efficient production and of gaining a profit expected by the founders.

Similar responses were to be had in areas such as product pricing, market orientation and motivation. In the early 1990s the prices of goods and services offered by the major public utilities were still being set by government bodies and consequently managers in these organizations often showed little awareness of the price mechanism. In contrast, outside of the public utilities there was a growing awareness of the impact of market competition on pricing. A chocolate manufacturer stated:

> The newcomers (foreign importers) are willing and able to apply market entry prices, and the domestic producers are prone to lose this battle.

Many managers, however, even though aware of the importance of pricing, were hampered by a lack of reliable cost information which made it extremely difficult to set competitive and profitable prices for products and services. Under the former system costing had not been regarded as a significant issue at enterprise level as enterprise accounts were subsumed within the accounting procedures for the overall national plan. After 1989, therefore, companies needed to account for the use and costs of inputs and furthermore develop and implement functioning costing systems.

With regard to the shift from a predominantly product orientation to a market orientation managers generally acknowledged the inherent weakness of a product-focused approach in the new conditions and the need for sales and marketing, although some managers had only a limited idea of what was actually required. A manager from a medical research institute commented, however, that:

> It is a fundamental requirement to reorganise the institute with special emphasis on trading and marketing activities. In short, turning the present research-orientated firm into a more market and trade conscious institute.

It was moreover evident that creating a pool of expert marketers would take some time. Furthermore, there appeared to be little change in the area of employee motivation as work performance in many industries was still largely undifferentiated, with few incentives for individuals to raise their own levels of performance. A manager from an oil and gas company noted in respect of the remuneration system:

> The present remuneration system is very old fashioned: there are categories of jobs according to qualification, job title and time spent at the organization. These factors determine salaries and wages for the job, not the person. There is no significant difference between employees of the same job, and no motivation towards better performance.

Further research was undertaken with Hungarian managers from a cross-section of companies in terms of size, activity and stage of restructuring in the period 1993–96 (Bőgel *et al.*, 1997). One characteristic that was repeatedly identified in this study was the proactivity displayed by managers in the organizations under investigation. Clearly, proactivity was not totally absent under the former regime but was fundamentally constrained by the general framework within which enterprises and their managers had to operate. This proactivity is particularly evident in the new small enterprises seeking to establish themselves and prosper in the face of substantial competition. In other cases this proactivity may be no more than the desperate response to the new circumstances, driven by a need for survival. If the ship is sinking (and many organizations appeared to fit this description), one can either leave (and many managers have) or one can stay on board in order to try to keep the ship afloat. This proactivity was frequently allied to a critical analysis of the company's situation and its capacity to respond adequately to the often rapidly changing situation. Many managers, particularly middle managers, felt frustrated at what they considered to be top management's inability to change quickly enough, to identify key deficiencies and develop appropriate strategies which might provide the necessary tangible and intangible resources and give the organization a better chance of survival.

Clearly, many top managements were torn between the security of the past and the unknown nature of the future and sought refuge in established forms of enterprise behaviour such as political lobbying and the pious hope that the state would continue to bale them out, even though post-1989 governments continually professed their commitment to the establishment of a market economy and the privatization of state-owned enterprises. In such cases it was commonplace for the more talented middle managers, particularly those with some experience of working in the West or knowledge of western management methods and with foreign language skills (especially English and German) to be lured away to another company (often a foreign company) or to set up on their own. This factor also helped to sustain the growth of small businesses, contributing in no small way to the transformation of the economy. At the same time it depleted the established enterprises of some of their more talented and go-ahead human resources.

A complementary picture is that of top managers who had assumed leading positions since the change of regime. Many had already been working for the company, in middle management or in leading technical positions, before assuming the mantle of managing director. Thrust into new positions these senior managers now had to identify and implement a new purpose for their organization. In conjunction with the issue of day-to-day survival the new MDs had to devote themselves to considerations of strategy in order to secure the future of their companies. It was no easy task to devise a workable strategy, given the intellectual and physical inheritance of the past and the general economic environment of rapid and fluid change. Yet these managers were prepared to wrestle long and hard with the challenges and threats facing their companies.

Proactivity was often accompanied by the realization that the organization now needed to function autonomously and by a sense of responsibility for its continued existence. With the dismantlement of the former system of economic management there was a clear intention, consistently expressed by the new democratic governments, to make companies autonomous within a specified framework of economic action in which companies themselves were conceived as the principal agents. Autonomy can be perceived as an opportunity to follow one's own goals and strategies, to develop without the constraints of the state and centralized planning. On the other hand autonomy can be a burden, a withdrawal of state support and the loss of a final refuge in the case of dire difficulties. While at least in theory liquidation became feasible towards the end of the former regime, it was never the ultimate arbiter of the fate of an enterprise, as reasons of state could always be called upon to overrule the exigencies of the 'market'. This has now all changed and companies really have to find their own way of survival.

This can be a demanding task for organizations created for specific purposes in a different system. They may clearly find it difficult to find a new purpose and scope, especially if their primary function derived from the way the economic system was structured in the past. Organizations such as the research institute and foreign trade organization investigated in Bőgel *et al.* (1997) had a specific function which was, however, frequently undermined by their client organizations' desire for autarky. With market liberalization such organizations were already being challenged by their former clients' own in-house organizations, even though they might initially have been only embryonic.

There may be a number of driving forces behind such a quest for a new purpose and scope, including a desire for survival, ambition to prove oneself in the new conditions, a belief in the validity and value of the company's activities. A further driving force is a sense of responsibility towards one's fellow employees and to the local community. The research institute was keen to preserve a body of talented and experienced research scientists; another company in the Bőgel *et al.* (1997) study was an engineering company in the town of Eger. It was the town's largest employer and had a large number of skilled engineers. Possession of such human resources was in itself not a sufficient condition for survival, but these specialist resources had to be substantially retained if these companies were to have any kind of future.

The issue of autonomy is therefore bound up with a range of other considerations – privatization, strategic purpose and scope and a broader social responsibility to employees and the local community. Many top managers in the study often appeared to be trying to 'square the circle', ensuring short-term survival, developing longer-term strategies, seeking out new customers and markets, developing new products, pursuing potential investors, keeping current creditors happy, maintaining as much employment as possible.

Economic transformation in Hungary has resulted in the 1990s in substantial organizational diversity as a result of the interaction of companies' desire to survive in and adapt to the new market environment, whilst at the same time retaining aspects of socialist identity (Gyekiczky and Haferkemper, 1996). This diversity has been intensified by the upsurge of new firms, the entry of numerous foreign investors and the presence in managerial positions of managers imbued with socialist and market ideologies (Gyekiczky and Haferkemper, 1996). Not surprisingly, traditional organizational cultures have persisted and influenced managerial attitudes and behaviours. Even though there has been substantial changes within senior management and considerable movement of managers within organizations, actual organizational change within Hungarian companies was somewhat limited in the early 1990s (Whitley and Czaban, 1998). Nevertheless, in comparison to the majority of other CEE countries, Hungary has developed a strongly entrepreneurial business culture which has also drawn on the legacy of the communist experiments in marketization and enterprise autonomy and found a resonance in Hungarians' propensity to individualism. With the acceleration of economic and corporate restructuring from the mid 1990s the influence of the socialist legacy has been undermined more consistently. These developments have moreover given greater scope to Hungarians' individualist and entrepreneurial inclinations.

References

Balaton, K. (1998) 'The Role of Management Executives in the Transformation Process in Hungary', in Lang, R. (ed.), *Management Executives in the East European Transformation Process*, Munich and Mering: Rainer Hampp Verlag, pp. 37–52.

Barratt Brown, M. (1984) *Models in Political Economy*, Harmondsworth: Penguin.

Bőgel, G., Edwards, V. and Wax, M. (1997) *Hungary Since Communism, The Transformation of Business*, Basingstoke and London: Macmillan.

Bőgel, G. and Huszty, A. (1999) 'Strategy-making in Hungary', in Edwards, V. (ed.), Proceedings of the Fifth Annual Conference on *The Impact of Transformation on Individuals, Organizations, Society*, Chalfont St Giles: CREEB, pp. 358–65.

Csapó, L. (1975) 'The Hungarian Reform, Towards a Planned, Guided Economy', in Kirschen, E. (ed.), *Economic Policies Compared: West and East, Vol 2: National and International Experiences*, Amsterdam and New York: North Holland/American Elsevier, pp. 60–142.

Dóbak, M. and Tari, E. (1996) 'Evolution of Organizational Forms in the Transition Period of Hungary', in *Journal for East European Management Studies*, 1, 2, pp. 7–35.

EBRD (1998) *Annual Report 1997*, London: EBRD.

Edwards, V. and Foster, F. (1994) 'Meeting the Need for Management Development in Eastern Europe', *The International Journal of Educational Management*, 8, 1, pp. 14–19.

Ehrlich, E. and Révész, G. (1995) *Hungary and its Prospects 1985–2005*, Budapest: Akadémiai Kiadó.

Falus Szikra, K. (1995) *The Position and Conditions of Intellectuals in Hungary*, Budapest: Akadémiai Kiadó.

Gyekiczky, T. and Haferkemper, M. (1996), 'Organisationswandel und Persistenz? Betriebliche Transformationspfade in Ungarn im Vergleich', in Lang, R. (ed.), *Wandel von Unternehmenskulturen in Ostdeutschland und Osteuropa*, Munich and Mering: Rainer Hampp Verlag, pp. 171–84.

Kiezun, W. (1991) *Management in Socialist Countries, USSR and Central Europe*, Berlin and New York: Walter de Gruyter.

Kornai, J. (1990) *The Socialist System*, Princeton: Princeton University Press.

Lawrence, P. (1998) *Issues in European Business*, Basingstoke and London: Routledge.

Pearce, J. (1993) 'From Socialism to Capitalism: The Effects of Hungarian Human Resources Practices', in Maruyama, M. (ed.), *Management Reform in Eastern and Central Europe*, Aldershot: Dartmouth, pp. 111–31.

Pető, I. (1990) 'Distinctive Features of the Hungarian Economy. Changes in its Workings from 1945 Onwards', in Kilényi, G. and Lamm, V. (eds), *New Tendencies in the Hungarian Economy*, Budapest: Akadémiai Kiadó, pp. 7–60.

Samli, A. and Jermakowicz, W. (1983) 'The Stages of Marketing Evolution in East European Countries', *European Journal of Marketing*, 17, 2, pp. 26–33.

Swain, N. (1992) *Hungary, The Rise and Fall of Feasible Socialism*, London: Verso.

Whitley, R. and Czaban, L. (1998) 'Institutional Transformation and Enterprise Change in an Emergent Capitalist Economy: The Case of Hungary', *Organization Studies*, 19, 2, pp. 259–80.

Wirtschaftslage und Reformprozesse in Mittel- und Osteuropa (1999), Berlin: Bundesministerium für Wirtschaft und Technologie.

Poland

Poland is the largest country in Central and Eastern Europe with a population of 38.6 million in 1996. Poland has been in the forefront of countries transforming their economies and economic organizations. Under communism Poland was possibly the most restive of the countries of CEE. Polish post-war history embodies various attempts by the Polish Communist Party to assert and maintain its control. During the communist period there had been periodic manifestations of revolt against the regime, including the Poznan uprising of 1956, the Gdansk riots of December 1970, the establishment of the trade union Solidarity (Solidarnosc) and further strikes in 1976 following an announcement of substantial increases in food prices. The difficulty of maintaining political stability in Poland can be exemplified by the number of heads of government. This turnover in Party leadership in the communist period was in sharp contrast to the majority of CEE countries which were typified by a long-term stability of the ruling elite. The culmination of the Party's attempts to achieve stable conditions in Poland was the imposition of martial law in December 1981. Communist Poland's last decade was thus characterized by a period of overt repression, followed by a process of negotiation leading to democratic elections in 1989, as a result of which the communist regime came to an end.

Polish thought and culture have been strongly influenced by a number of factors. Poland was a great imperial power from the fifteenth to the seventeenth centuries and the empire's territories extended at one time into modern-day Lithuania, Belarus and the Ukraine. The University of Cracow, one of the oldest in Europe, had already been founded in 1364. Copernicus, born in Torun in 1473, was the founder of modern astronomy, pronouncing that the Sun, and not the Earth, was the centre of our planetary system. It was furthermore the Polish king Jan Sobieski who in 1683 stopped the Ottoman advance into Europe by defeating the Sultan's forces at the gates of Vienna. Poland thus played a pivotal role in the course of European history and culture.

The Polish experience is also distinguished by the fall from greatness and the three-way partition of Poland between Prussia, Russia and Austria in the eighteenth century. By 1795, following the third partition, Poland had disappeared as a sovereign state, having shown itself unable to withstand the attacks of aggressive neighbours: Swedes to the north, Austrians to the south, Prussians to the west and Russians to the east. The relations with its western and eastern neighbours proved particularly critical, and Poland was sandwiched between the two states that were intent on expanding into and annexing Polish territories.

A key distinguishing feature of Polish society has been its relationship with the Catholic Church. Religious affiliation distinguished the Catholic Poles from the predominantly Lutheran Prussians and the Orthodox Russians. The Catholic Church served as a haven of traditional Polish values under the foreign occupations of the nineteenth and early twentieth centuries and more recently under communism. The election to the Papacy in 1978 of Karol Wojtyla, Archbishop of Cracow, as Pope John Paul II gave a further boost to Catholic Poles in their resistance to communism.

Modern Poland was refounded in 1918 after the First World War. Poles, however, comprised only around 70 per cent of the population which included large minorities of Ukrainians, Belorussians, Germans, Lithuanians and Jews (Wiskemann, 1966). Both Germany and the newly established Soviet Union were hostile to the new Polish state. Many Germans resented the inclusion of German minorities in Poland, the establishment of a Polish corridor to the Baltic, separating East Prussia from the rest of Germany and the status of Danzig (Gdansk) as a free city under the aegis of the League of Nations. The Soviet Union resented Poland's acquisition of territories formerly part of the Russian Empire and populated largely by Ukrainians and Belorussians. A war between Poland and the Soviet Union in 1919–20 was concluded by the defeat of the Soviet army outside Warsaw.

Poland's new found independence, however, did not last long. On 1st September 1939 the German army invaded Poland; shortly afterwards Soviet forces moved into eastern Poland, seizing territories as agreed in a pact between Hitler and Stalin. The German occupation during the Second World War brought enormous suffering and hardship to the population, including atrocities against civilians and the systematic extermination of the Jews. The Soviet annexation of Eastern Poland and the subsequent Soviet advance into German-occupied territory also involved considerable brutality.

Cultural values

The main cultural values have evolved over a period of substantial turbulence, including imperial greatness, decline, partition and the loss of nationhood and the more recent re-establishment of an independent Poland.

In general Polish culture is marked by a strong vein of individualism. Individuals tend to be assertive and self-promoting. A negative manifestation of this is a lack of enthusiasm to work in a disciplined way and a reluctance to take part in activities involving cooperation with others (Podgorecki, 1993:27). An extension of this trait is the construction of personal facades, underlining the importance of appearance over substance (op. cit.:23).

Individualism goes hand in hand with a marked egalitarianism based on the former equality of all members of the Polish nobility irrespective of their individual power and wealth. The negative manifestation of this egalitarianism is an envy of, rather than respect for, the achievements of others (op. cit.:18).

A third characteristic is what Podgorecki (1993:24) describes as an 'attitude of spectacular principledness' which is reserved for extraordinary situations of national life such as the quest to regain national independence, the struggle against oppressors, and so on. In 1939 Polish mounted cavalry attempted to repel German tank units. The widespread support for Solidarity under the communist regime could also be interpreted as a manifestation of this cultural value.

Fourth, reflecting more the peasant dimension of Polish society, there is a reliance on family and friends which evolved during the periods of insecurity and foreign occupation. Family and friends provided mutual contacts and support at times when more impersonal relationships were neither available nor trusted. This reliance on personal contacts has evolved into the extensive use of informal networks operating outside or alongside official channels of communication and authority. In their more degenerate form these informal relationships have been described as 'dirty togetherness' (op. cit.:18). This aspect of Polish culture was given further impetus under communism because of the inherent shortages of the economic system and the limited control individuals in general had over the exercise of political power.

Finally, there is an absence of an entrepreneurial tradition in the sense of initiating and implementing economic activities. The Polish middle class which developed in the nineteenth century was engaged predominantly in administrative and professional activities. This cultural disregard for entrepreneurial activities is portrayed by Sikorski (1998:238):

> Poles, at least in the self-image of our cultural elites, remained unsullied by trade – and Communism prolonged this blissful detachment. Penniless intelligentsia remained at the top of the social hierarchy, as noble in opposition to Communism as their gentry grandfathers had been in opposition to the czars, and just as inept . . . Money was an awkward subject for them.

The demise of the communist regime has in many ways served as an antidote to this traditional 'relaxed' attitude to entrepreneurial activity. There is now considerable evidence of a developing class of especially young entrepreneurs who are devoted to making a success of their business activities and measuring this success in financial terms.

Poland in 1945 after the conclusion of the Second World War was significantly different from its pre-war predecessor. Geographically it had moved westward; in the west the border with Germany was now formed by the rivers Oder and Neisse; Poland obtained substantial territories from Germany (Pomerania, Silesia and southern East Prussia) while in the east it lost territory to the Soviet Union (western Ukraine, western Belorussia and parts of Lithuania including the capital Vilnius). Poland now had a long coastline with major seaports; it was geographically compact and the population was overwhelmingly Polish. The vast majority of the Jewish population had perished during the Holocaust; the German population fled or was expelled; most members of the eastern minorities (Ukrainians, Belorussians and Lithuanians) were incorporated in the Soviet Union.

Poland had suffered enormously during the Second World War. In the early post-war period there was an immense need to rebuild the devastated cities and towns, settle the territories vacated by their German inhabitants and in general to reconstruct the Polish economy. Moreover, Poland in 1945 now found itself within the Soviet sphere of influence, with the result that political and economic practice followed the Soviet model. Under communism Poland changed from being a largely agricultural, rural society to being an industrial and urban one. Before the Second World War industry accounted for less than one third of gross national income. By 1979 it was two thirds. In 1950 just over a third of the population lived in urban settlements; by 1989 it was just over 60 per cent (Hardy and Rainnie, 1996:34). However, the implementation of the Soviet model and the introduction of communism in Poland occurred in the context of the Polish culture and the history of Polish-Russian relations. For the Russians Poland had been the route of entry into Russia used by a number of invaders (e.g. Napoleon and Hitler). For the Poles Russia had been an occupier and was now imposing its ideology on Poland. Furthermore, the strong tradition of belief in Catholicism made it difficult for many Poles to accept the atheism inherent in communist ideology. These tensions were never really resolved in the period 1945–89. The Polish Communist Party was one of the weakest in CEE and '– even during the Stalinist phase – the most reluctant to identify fully with the Soviet model' (Arnason, 1993:147).

The Polish experience of communist economic management differed in some significant aspects from the Soviet model and from the experience of other CEE countries, even though general features such as nationalization of firms and central planning were introduced and in general enterprises had clear functional structures and were managed in a marked hierarchical manner. One major difference, which distinguished Poland from its COMECON neighbours, was the persistence of private ownership in agriculture. Collectivization of agriculture was abandoned in Poland in 1956. Throughout the communist period over 80 per cent of agricultural land remained in private ownership (Lavigne, 1999:9), even though private farms had to operate within the framework of the state-run system and suffered various types of discrimination in the form of access to farming inputs and materials and the level of administered prices.

Second, Poland was characterized by more open worker opposition to the official system as well as by more effective worker organization culminating in the formation of the Solidarity trade union. Workers' councils had first been set up spontaneously at the time of the Poznan riots in the summer of 1956 although their influence was quickly diluted (Petkov and Thirkell, 1991:181). In the early 1980s Solidarity sought to revive the role of the workers' council, in particular its right to elect enterprise directors (op. cit.:190–191). Whatever their actual influence the workers' councils testified to the existence of workers' interests as a distinct social category and gave at least the impression that workers exercised a certain authority over the way enterprises were managed. More clearly than in any of the other countries of CEE there was in Poland an open divergence of Communist Party and worker interests. This was an interesting feature from the standpoint of the official ideology according to which the Communist Party was the de facto representative of working class interests and acted as the vanguard of the working class. Workers' councils, moreover, continued to play a significant role in the process of privatization after 1989.

Third, the Polish economy was increasingly opened up to the global economy from the early 1970s as the government, following the 1970 Gdansk riots, sought to buy off popular dissatisfaction by using western credits to fund a rising standard of living for the population. This policy created an increasing level of indebtedness to western creditors. The level of Polish indebtedness soared from US$1.1 billion in 1971 to US$20.5 billion in 1979. In terms of total East European indebtedness the Polish share rose from 12 per cent to 30 per cent over the same period (Aldcroft and Morewood, 1995:161).

The opening to the world economy was, however, not entirely negative. In general, Poland under communism had demonstrated a greater degree of openness than many of its partners in COMECON. Many of these external links were of a personal nature, for example, with Polish émigré communities in the United States and France; there were also academic contacts with western universities. In the economic sphere some companies had been permitted to liaise directly with foreign partners, rather than use the services of centralized import-export organizations. These companies were able to acquire a certain expertise in dealing with foreign partners and in foreign environments. Moreover, there were a number of foreign-Polish joint ventures operating in Poland itself such as the one with FIAT, using technology which was considered superseded in western Europe to produce Polski FIATs for the domestic and foreign markets.

The range of contacts with foreign partners and the exposure to foreign, particularly west European and American markets and practices, gave those Polish firms involved in such activities a certain edge over other Polish firms limited to operating in the domestic arena (Hardy and Rainnie, 1996). Such an advantage was to become especially beneficial when Poland began to establish a market economy. One of Kewell's (1997) case study companies was a manufacturer of farm equipment and agricultural machinery in south-east Poland. Although manufacturing primarily for the Polish market, the enterprise exported around 20 per cent of its output to continental western Europe and Scandinavia. Towards the end of the communist regime the enterprise entered into a joint venture with a consortium of Italian companies, with the aim of expanding its product range and increasing its presence and credibility in western markets. The joint venture did not come to fruition because of incompatible expectations and lack of trust. In spite of this the Polish company's chairman commented (Kewell, 1997:150):

> In my view a lot of mistakes were made during the negotiations of the deal. But then it was 1988 and the economy was centrally planned. It was a real challenge to go into business with foreign investors. I think that our potential success was just beginning in 1988 and our early experience at dealing with very advanced methods of management, marketing and sales techniques is why we are successful right now.

The socialist manager in Poland

Managers in communist Poland (Kozinski and Listvan, 1993) shared many of the characteristics of the typical socialist manager. The vast majority were engineering graduates and members of the Communist Party. Managers enjoyed neither high status nor prestige and received relatively low remuneration. According to Kozinski and Listvan (1993:201), 'In 1986, the average wage of a coal miner was 34 per cent higher than a nationwide directorial salary', although managers had privileged access to a range of scarce goods.

Traditional cultural values, moreover, can be seen in the way managers were regarded and in the way they operated. The low status of managers can be explained to a large degree by the traditional avoidance of entrepreneurial activities. Managers themselves, however, were driven by an urge to achieve success and wished to operate independently. At the same time this cultural individualism was counter-balanced by a certain egalitarianism as manifested in the operation of the workers' councils. Individualism and self-advancement were thus accompanied by a certain regard for the opinions and views of other parties.

Kozinski and Listvan (1993:91) describe the effective general manager: 'An effective general manager was a person successful in attaining money, raw materials, equipment, energy, and workforce.' This description accords well with descriptions of general managers in other CEE countries. Effectiveness, from the viewpoint of the workforce, was determined not so much by achieving targets but by assuring the means to achieve the targets and smoothing the work of the employees.

The effectiveness of the general manager therefore depended to some degree on influencing the allocation process, using his political contacts to ensure adequacy of materials. Key enterprises in strategic sectors of the economy enjoyed particular influence over political bodies. At the local level too senior managers could play an important role, interrelating with the local Nomenklatura, the leading stratum of the Communist Party, in a situation of expected mutual benefits (Domanski, 1997:34).

In spite of low status and prestige senior managers in particular exercised considerable influence as their enterprises, in addition to providing employment, controlled access to other benefits (for example, housing and certain scarce consumer goods) and could influence the allocation of resources. With the emergence of Solidarity in the early 1970s managers also had to deal on a daily basis with one of the main opponents of the existing communist regime. Because of this managers also performed a sensitive political function.

After communism

The years preceding the demise of communism in 1989 were betokened by persistent crisis and uncertainty. Economic reforms introduced towards the end of 1988 under Prime Minister Ratowski increased the autonomy of enterprise managers, for example, in dealing with suppliers. The reforms were intended to improve the efficiency of the economic system, by creating quasi-market conditions in which enterprises were supposed to operate. However, 'market socialism' was not envisaged to lead to the actual privatization of state-owned enterprises.

A side effect of the Ratowski reforms was the phenomenon of so-called 'spontaneous privatization' which resulted in the illegal sale of enterprise assets to members of the Nomenklatura (Kewell, 1997:11–12). A new group of capitalists was thus actually created under the former communist regime from those managers with Nomenklatura status who had in some ways foreseen the direction of political events.

The end of the communist regime turned the world of the state-owned enterprises upside down. The old securities, underpinned by subsidies and reliefs, centralized investments and excessive demand, gave way to great insecurity often leading to paralysis. Enterprises were now faced with declining demand, loss of state support, bankruptcy, market forces and domestic and foreign competition (Golebiowski, 1997:203). The structure of the economy began to change rapidly. There was a rapid fall in industrial output for a relatively short period but economic growth resumed in 1992 (Poland was the first of the former command economies to come out of decline). By mid 1996 the private sector accounted for 60 per cent of GDP. The structure of GDP, moreover, had changed from being dominated by industry to being dominated by services. In the period 1989–95 industry's share of GDP fell from 44 to 29 per cent; services' share rose from 30 to 53 per cent. Over the same period there was a considerable reorientation of Polish trade, with Germany becoming Poland's leading trading partner as well as a major foreign investor (PAIZ, 1997).

However, notwithstanding its brevity, the period immediately following the establishment of the new democratic government was dominated by the experience of 'Shock Therapy' resulting from the impact of Finance Minister Balcerowicz's plan to solve Poland's hyper-inflation (Blazyca, 1997:65). At the end of 1989 monthly inflation exceeded 30 per cent, and the aim of the plan was to defeat inflation and establish a market economy. As a result of the Balcerowicz Plan unemployment soared, demand plummeted (eliminating shortages) and in spite of the difficult circumstances the private sector expanded. In contrast, however, many state-owned enterprises responded to Shock Therapy by adopting a defensive posture designed to protect their position and interests (Kewell, 1997:22).

There also developed a certain opposition to privatization, partly fuelled by a reaction against Nomenklatura capitalism, the perceived interests of state-enterprise managers, accusations of corruption and political failures (op. cit.:21). Privatization thus progressed more slowly than initially expected and involved a number of mechanisms (Blazyca, 1997). Some companies were acquired by foreign investors, others by a combination of workers and managers, whilst a large group of companies were taken out of direct state ownership, their assets passing into the control of state banks ('restructuring banks') as a precursor to full-blown privatization. The market economy in Poland over the 1990s retained therefore a strong element of state involvement and the landscape of firms is relatively varied with old and new private firms, foreign-owned firms, state-controlled firms and firms resulting from the Nomenklatura privatizations.

Initially, many established features of the former regime proved resistant to change. Even though managers asserted management's prerogative to manage, there was also a reluctance to implement mass redundancies, necessary because of the overmanning under communism, and many senior managers saw themselves as 'sympathetic advocates of workers' interests' (Kewell, 1997:111). This was particularly the case in those 'unrestructured' enterprises which still had functioning workers' councils. Great hope was placed in external sources of salvation such as privatization and FDI. However, the deteriorating economic circumstances of many enterprises forced cuts in jobs and wages. Many employees felt betrayed; there were accusations that management was 'feathering its own nest' (op. cit.:113) and giving in to personal loyalties rather than adopting more objective measures of individual capabilities (op. cit.:138). The latter accusation can be seen as a persistence of traditional cultural values and the lack of differentiation between life at work and life outside work. Especially in smaller towns people interrelate both as managers and employees and as family, friends and neighbours (Robinson and Tomczak-Stepien, 1998:126).

Western managers, moreover, found it 'very difficult to get the local management to take responsibility' (Kewell, 1997:144). One western manager interviewed in mid 1994 was scathing of the senior managers in a plant run by their local partners in eastern Poland:

> There's definitely no measure of accountability. A manager here is somebody who comes with his shirt and tie on and sits behind a desk in his management office and people feed him bits of information on a very formal basis. You have meetings with town councils, ministers, all sorts of things but you don't actually have to get out into the factory and find out how to make it better (Kewell, 1997:141).

Such a view of Polish management is clearly partial and underlines the approach of senior managers clinging to attitudes and practices which appear typical of the former regime. This possibility for such practices to persist was reflected in the varied yet changing landscape of Polish firms. Changes in management attitudes and practice are portrayed by Rozanski and Sikorski (1996) who have reported on research they conducted in three recent periods of time in Polish firms. The first investigation was conducted between 1986 and 1990. The vast majority of firms, largely because of financial constraints, were involved in a process of rationalization or of upgrading products and processes. At most only 15 per cent of firms surveyed were undertaking what might be regarded as real entrepreneurial activities such as new product and market development. A subsequent survey in 1992–93 revealed no significant changes, which the authors attribute to company directors' reluctance to change and the widespread traditional attitude of risk aversion.

By 1994 Rozanski and Sikorski (1996) identified some changes in attitudes, reflecting the increasing influence of the external environment. Although the overwhelming majority of managers in their study (between 80 and 90 per cent) concentrated on solving company problems, a small minority (between 10 and 20 per cent) were now paying greater attention to seeking and developing opportunities outside their firms. This was particularly evident in areas such as purchasing and supply, although as yet there were few signs of marketing activity.

A further project conducted between 1993 and 1995 by Rozanski and Sikorski (1996) indicated an increasing influence of external forces such as markets and competition. This influence was clearly changing the context of decision making, with a shift from a focus on production to the elaboration of more qualitative aims such as product quality and customer satisfaction.

Rozanski and Sikorski (1996) also brought to light other developments. Private companies in particular were being managed by professional managers (rather than political appointees). Managers were also becoming much younger with many aged between 30 and 35. Headhunting was commonplace, indicating a shortage of top-quality managers. On the negative side, there was evidence of an increased intensity in the pace and scope of work, with many managers suffering from burn-out.

Rozanski and Sikorski's (1996) research emphasizes the evolution of managerial practices and behaviours as companies respond to the changes in the economic system. Clearly these responses are not uniform and it is possible for 'old-style' enterprises and market-driven companies to co-exist, at least in the shorter term. Boerner (1998) relates changes in management style and organizational culture to the switch from the closed society of the former regime to the open society which succeeded it. Up to the 1982 reforms Polish enterprises had been managed in a largely autocratic manner. Subsequently, there had been an increasing 'openness' in the way in which enterprises had been managed; this 'openness' had accelerated since 1989. Increasing openness, however, was also associated with conflicts, problems of coordination and possible inefficiencies and led to an increasing demand for counter-measures providing a degree of stability and security. Such a view could be interpreted as a reaction against the excesses of the process of marketization and as a desire to retain elements of the former system. In consequence it is not so surprising that some components of the former style of management have persisted even in newly formed companies, as there is a widespread view that companies and their managers need to underpin the openness of the market system with features of the former system which support individual security. In their drive for competitiveness and innovation companies thus also need to bear in mind their employees' need for order and stability.

In conclusion

Management in today's Poland displays a diversity of forms, with old and new practices co-existing. The presence of particular practices is not necessarily correlated with the origins and nature of the firm. It is possible to find old-style autocratic management in newly founded firms. It is also possible to find newer managerial approaches in firms which are still fundamentally in the state sector since firms which are yet to be privatized are possibly under greater pressure to survive. There is thus no simple correlation between firm type and managerial style.

According to Kostera *et al.* (Kostera, 1995; Kostera *et al.*, 1995; Kostera and

Wicha, 1996) there was considerable variety in the responses of companies and their managers to the change of economic system. Although the overall rationale of companies after 1989 was economic rather than political as under communism, this did not signify that political forms of activity were no longer effective. In fact Kostera (1995:674) notes that 'There is still considerable scope for survival by means of political lobbying and engaging in party politics . . .' Even though many managers who had worked under communism appear to articulate the discourse of western management, Kostera intimates that many of them actually continued to operate in the 'wait-and-see' manner prevalent under communism (Kostera *et al.*, 1995).

Factors which are in general more conducive to change are foreign ownership or involvement as well as high management turnover (particularly if this involves younger professional managers). Change tends to be inhibited if the company is still managed by 'old-style' managers and if company ownership has passed into the hands of insiders, particularly the pre-1989 top management. It is not surprising therefore that many companies are still organized in a traditional functional manner and the managerial style tends to be autocratic.

However, there is a marked change in the balance of manager–worker relations, irrespective of firm type. The balance moreover has shifted substantially to the benefit of management. The influence of workers' councils persisted after 1989 but in general only for as long as it took the enterprise to be privatized. The process of restructuring too generally disadvantages the labour force. Many managers have on the other hand benefitted financially from the process of privatization, becoming owners of company assets.

The introduction of the market economy has encouraged entrepreneurism and entrepreneurial activity. As previously mentioned, there is evidence that business is an activity which currently enjoys social status and that a vibrant business class is developing. Although managers are still predominantly male, the new group of Polish managers is considerably younger than were their counterparts under communism.

Furthermore, the environment of the market economy is an environment conducive to the Polish cultural characteristic of individualism. In the current circumstances there are opportunities for Polish managers to make their mark, to set up their own businesses, to aspire to become rich. In this regard the development of Polish management since 1989 has been strongly influenced by the American model of management. Many Polish managers have studied in the United States or have studied for American MBAs in Poland. The perceived success of American management is clearly influential. Kewell (1997:156) notes the appointment of a former professor of economics to the position of managing director on account of his 'missionary zeal for western (mostly American) theories of management'. This American influence, however, is both supported and counterbalanced by more traditional Polish cultural values.

References

Aldcroft, D. and Morewood, S. (1995) *Economic Change in Eastern Europe since 1918*, Aldershot: Edward Elgar.

Arnason, J. (1993) The *Future that Failed, Origins and Destinies of the Soviet Model*, London: Routledge.

Blazyca, G. (1997) 'The Business Culture in Poland', in Bateman, M. (ed.), *Business Cultures in Central & Eastern Europe*, Oxford: Butterworth-Heinemann, pp. 60–87.

Boerner, S. (1998) 'Transformation als Führung in die offene Gesellschaft – Ergebnisse einer empirischen Untersuchung in polnischen Betrieben', in Lang, R. (ed.), *Führungskräfte im osteuropäischen Transformationsprozeß*, III. Chemnitzer Ostforum, Munich and Mering: Rainer Hampp, pp. 209–225.

Domanski, B. (1997) *Industrial Control over the Socialist Town, Benevolence or Exploitation?*, Westport, Connecticut and London: Praeger.

Golebiowski, J. (1997) 'Adjustment of the Polish Corporate Sector to Market Economics', in Lubinski, M. (ed.), *Poland, International Economic Report 1996/1997*, Warsaw School of Economics, pp. 203–207.

Hardy, J. and Rainnie, A. (1996) *Restructuring Krakow, Desperately Seeking Capitalism*, London: Mansell.

Kewell, B. (1997) 'Nation Without a State, Managers Without Management? A Study of Organisational Change in Post-socialist Poland, 1989–1994' Ph.D. thesis, Buckinghamshire College of Higher Education/Brunel University.

Kostera, M. (1995) 'Differing Managerial Responses to Change in Poland', *Organization Studies*, 16/4, pp. 673–97.

Kostera, M., Proppé, M. and Szatkowski, M. (1995) 'Staging the New Romantic Hero in the Old Cynical Theatre: On Managers, Roles and Change in Poland', *Journal of Organizational Behavior*, 16, pp. 631–46.

Kostera, M. and Wicha, M. (1996) 'The "Divided Self" of Polish State-owned Enterprises: The Culture of Organizing', *Organization Studies*, 17/1, pp. 93–105.

Kozinski, J. and Listvan, T. (1993) 'Poland', in Peterson, R. (ed.), *Managers and National Culture, A Global Perspective*, Westport, Connecticut: Quorum Books, pp. 78–208.

Lavigne, M. (1999) *The Economics of Transition, From Socialist Economy to Market Economy*, Basingstoke and London: Macmillan, 2nd ed.

PAIZ (1997) *Poland, Fundamental Facts, Figures and Regulations*, April, Polish Agency for Foreign Investment.

Petkov, K. and Thirkell, J. (1991) *Labour Relations in Eastern Europe, Organisational Design and Dynamics*, London: Routledge.

Podgorecki, A. (1993) 'Polish Traditions and Perspectives of Post-socialist Reforms', in Mayurama, M. (ed.), *Management Reform in Eastern and Central Europe, Use of Pre-communist Cultures*, Aldershot: Dartmouth, pp. 13–43.

Robinson, I. and Tomczak-Stepien, B. (1998) 'Appraising Business Culture in Post-Socialist Polish Firms', in Edwards, V. (ed.), Proceedings of the Fourth Annual Conference on *Convergence or Divergence: Aspirations and Reality in Central and Eastern Europe and Russia*, Chalfont St Giles: CREEB, pp. 115–131.

Rozanski, J. and Sikorski, A. (1996) 'Polnische Unternehmen und ihre Führungskräfte im kulturellen Wandel zur Zeit der wirtschaftlichen Transformation in Polen', in Lang, R. (ed.), *Wandel von Unternehmenskulturen in Ostdeutschland und Osteuropa*, II. Chemnitzer Ostforum, Munich and Mering: Rainer Hampp, pp. 185–94.

Sikorski, R. (1998) *The Polish House, An Intimate History of Poland*, London: Orion Books.

Wiskemann, E. (1966) *Europe of the Dictators 1919–1945*, London: Collins.

CHAPTER 4

Russia

Russian managers' experience of the collapse of the communist system in the early 1990s has been particularly acute, for a number of reasons. The Soviet system of economic management had since 1917 functioned as the model of organizing economic activity in the socialist states. By the end of the 1980s, when the communist regimes of CEE began to collapse, the Soviet model had been in place in the Soviet Union for over 70 years. There were therefore few people still alive with any memory or experience of pre-1917 forms of economic organization. Russia, moreover, had changed substantially from a predominantly agricultural and in many respects despotic state to one which had developed a significant heavy industrial and military base.

Furthermore, although the collapse of the communist regimes in CEE had been accelerated (even facilitated) by Soviet President Gorbachev's reforms of the 1980s, these reforms (encapsulated by the terms *glasnost* and *perestroika*) had not actually been intended to do anything more than reform the existing system. It may be argued that Gorbachev's approach contained an inherent contradiction and that the outcome of the collapse of the Soviet system was as a consequence inevitable. It was, however, Gorbachev's successor, Boris Yeltsin, who took the actual step of terminating the Soviet system and establishing a political democracy and a market economy in 1992. Although the Soviet Union (and at its core Russia) had been the very instigator of the undermining of the Soviet system, the former Soviet Union took on the political and economic reforms at a later time than most of the countries of CEE. These reforms, moreover, also entailed the demise of the Soviet Union itself and the establishment of sovereign and truly independent states in Eastern Europe and Central Asia.

Even taking into consideration the secession of the republics from the Soviet Union, Russia is by all accounts a very large state, both in terms of population (*circa* 150m) and area (just over 17 million square kilometres). Russia stretches from the Baltic Sea to within a short distance of Alaska and Japan. The size of Russia, and more significantly the disregard by the former system of economic management of issues relating to geographical distance, were important factors which managers and firms had to face. Whereas, for example, energy costs had been largely ignored under the former system, these now assumed major importance so that geographical distance – and the costs of transportation – were no longer an issue which could simply be disregarded, as they impinged directly on economic activity.

A further significant dimension of the collapse of the Soviet Union was psychological. The Soviet Union had been a superpower (at least in political terms). World politics since 1945 had largely revolved around the struggle for supremacy between the Soviet Union and the United States, each acting as the leading representative of its respective political and economic system. This struggle manifested itself in a number of ways, including the 'space race' (which the Soviet Union initially won by launching the first unmanned and manned spacecraft – in 1957 and 1961 respectively) and the quest to win the allegiance of former European colonies in Africa, Asia and South America.

Within the former Soviet Union and in CEE Russia was the dominant power. The collapse of the Soviet Union and the communist system was perceived by many Russians in a way which was different from that of their CEE counterparts. For many Russians the transformation signified a loss of status and prestige, a reduction in global standing. From being leaders in the political and economic spheres, many Russians saw themselves diminished (and to a degree humiliated) through the collapse of the Soviet Union and having to relinquish the political and economic system which had been in operation since 1917.

Distinctive features of the former system

What were the distinguishing features of the system of economic management in Russia following the revolution of 1917? First, the process of developing and implementing the system was based solely on the blueprint outlined and elaborated over a number of decades by socialist writers. There were, however, no practical applications to imitate and adapt. In this respect the Russian case was truly unique and experimental.

Second, in the period 1917–45, the Russian experiment was carried out overwhelmingly in isolation as the vast majority of countries, especially the advanced market economies, abhorred and sought to undermine developments in Russia and, to a certain extent, feared that capitalism might actually succumb to communism. This fear was particularly acute after the end of World War I in 1918 when there were widespread communist revolutions in Europe. This experience of isolation, of struggling against overwhelming odds, was consequently a persistent feature of the Russian people's experience.

Third, the original implementation of the system in 1917 and thereafter occurred in a period of enormous turmoil in the political and economic spheres in Russia. In the political arena there was the overturning of the Tsarist system and civil war (including intervention by foreign powers). In the economic area there was the establishment of the new system of economic management in industry and agriculture, forced industrialization (with an emphasis on heavy industry) and widespread expropriations of private property. Especially under Stalin the new system was betokened by the widespread and often arbitrary use of terror – to eliminate individuals and groups regarded as inimical to the system or to the way in which it was evolving.

Notwithstanding enormous difficulties and distortions, the new system was able to demonstrate significant achievements. Russia became a significant economic and political power. A substantial economic base was established, with a particular emphasis on the energy and capital goods sectors. Politically, the new system overcame internal opposition and played a significant role in defeating Nazi Germany in the Second World War (1939–45). From being an international pariah in 1917 the Soviet Union had by 1945 become one of the world's leading Great Powers and by the 1950s the Soviet Union and the USA were unquestionably the global superpowers.

Interestingly, the practice of management and also economic organization under communism were strongly influenced by the apparent successes of American capitalism. The practice of Russian management was modelled in particular on Taylorist and Fordist approaches to industrial organization with their focus on fragmentation of tasks, strict organization, automation and mass production. Stalin even defined Leninism in the mid 1920s as a combination of 'Russian revolutionary sweep' and 'American efficiency' (Arnason, 1993:118). Russian management practice thus derived much of its inspiration from a style of management which is often regarded as seeking to treat individuals as if they were machines or automata. A further aspect of this American influence was the tendency to gigantism whereby only large scale, often very large scale, projects were given priority. Kotkin (1995) extensively describes one of many such projects, the construction of the Magnitogorsk steel complex in the southern Urals. The development and construction of Magnitogorsk involved using the services of a Chicago-based engineering company. The project was launched in 1926 and the first steel was produced in 1933 (Kotkin, 1995:54).

This fragmentation of activities as typified by Taylorism had a further attraction for the Soviet political elite. Coordination of economic activities was not the responsibility of general managers or owners, as in market economies, but lay in the hands of political appointees whose task it was to ensure that industrial organizations strove for and achieved the goals set for them by the Communist Party.

In 1917, the year of the Russian Revolution, Russia had had a predominantly agricultural economy. 80 per cent of the population lived at that time in rural areas. Industrial activities had been located in a limited number of geographical areas. Moscow, for example, had been developing into a significant industrial centre from the middle of the nineteenth century and a more widespread industrialization had been officially encouraged from towards the end of that century.

The period from 1917 up to the early 1970s witnessed a substantial expansion of the Soviet Union's industrial capacity and output, although there has been considerable debate about the reliability of official Soviet data (Lavigne, 1999:44–45). By 1950, moreover, the Soviet Union had become heavily industrialized. Over 60 per cent of national income was then being generated by the industry and construction sector (Lavigne, 1999:53).

The Red Executive

David Granick's (1960) portrayal of Russian enterprise directors was in many respects sympathetic and highlighted many of the similarities in the ways in which American and Russian directors operated. Granick recognized the role of the Communist Party not only in the overall management of the economy, but also in endowing company directors with the legitimacy to run their enterprises. The relationship to the Party was, however, a two-edged sword in that it encompassed both rewards (financial rewards and prestige) and obligations (for example, directors could be transferred by the Party).

Appointment to an enterprise directorship was not purely a party political decision. Enterprise directors were generally graduates (often in a technical subject) and had administrative experience. The enterprise director was also expected to be a decision-maker insofar as the achievement of the enterprise plan was concerned. The complexities and inefficiencies of the planning system, moreover, gave enterprise managers considerable scope to apply their creativity and decision-making skills. On the other hand, true innovations were discouraged as, in spite of possible long-term benefits, they might lead to disruptions of economic activity in the short term and hence cause the enterprise not to achieve its planning targets (Smith, 1976:287). One of the results of the system's weaknesses was a continuous high intensity of activity to ensure targets were met (for example, utilizing plant to high levels of capacity and frequent catching up on lost production – so-called 'storming').

Being an enterprise director required considerable interpersonal skills. The enterprise director was not an independent decision-maker and, to be successful, had to work positively with the enterprise's Party secretary, the enterprise Trades Union chairman and the director's own immediate superior as well as other politically significant persons. Even though this circle of close associates was imbued with the same ideological viewpoint, any disruption of the working relationship could have negative implications for the company director. For example, it could lead to transfer to another enterprise or, in certain circumstances, criminal proceedings.

Whilst being subject to overall political control and considerable pressures at work, enterprise directors enjoyed considerable privileges in the form of bonuses, accommodation and holiday opportunities. Such privileges were in sharp contrast to the general standard of life of the majority of the population and there was consequently a great deal of resentment of 'the bosses in the black Volgas' (Smith, 1976:278).

The establishment of the market economy

Russia had been undertaking a number of economic reforms since the mid 1980s. However, the economic reform package introduced by the government in 1992 signalled the rapid and in many respects extreme transformation of the Russian economy.

By the mid 1980s it was evident that only a radical transformation of Russia's political institutions could remedy the failings of the economic system. The growth rates of national income had been declining since the 1950s, with the decline accelerating from the mid 1970s. By the latter half of the 1980s the Soviet economy seemed to be coming to a standstill (Lavigne, 1999:58). In an attempt to make the Soviet socialist system operate effectively, Gorbachev began a comprehensive process of reforms.

The beginning of the changes which brought the Russian economy on to the path of the so-called transformation process from the centrally planned economy to the market can be dated as beginning in 1987, when two fundamental pieces of legislation were passed. One was the Law on State Enterprises, another the Law on Cooperatives. The former expanded considerably the autonomy of enterprises, the latter the autonomy of individuals (Gaddy 1996:63). However, traditional elements of the system, such as the soft budget constraint, state ownership of enterprise assets and state-controlled prices, remained intact. Enterprises continued to receive thousands of indicators and requests to fulfil hundreds of different monthly, quarterly and annual forms of bureaucratic inventiveness. In fact the then new Five Year Plan for 1986–90 was still being prepared on the basis of old assumptions and using the same traditional indicators.

Enterprises accustomed to limited independence were naturally keen to exploit (and abuse) the new opportunities granted them by the law, that is, of setting their own salaries and wages, and of converting the balances of the enterprises into cash. This situation, where on the one hand there continued to be tight state control over prices and on the other hand there was an opportunity for enterprises and individuals to increase cash incomes, could have only one outcome – severe monetary overhang. The result of this situation was shortages in almost everything, but most striking of all, in foodstuffs. Queues became a common feature of everyday life throughout the Soviet Union and 'where there is no queue there is nothing on the shelves' (Dyker, 1992:172).

In 1991 the Soviet leaders officially admitted for the first time the existence of inflation in the economic system. In fact it was running at 140 per cent a year. The government moved to revitalize the economy by giving incentives to enterprises facing problems 'such as the inconsistency between the *de jure* state ownership of most productive assets and *de facto* management control of most enterprise activities' (Ernst *et al.*, 1996:214). However, the inertia of the old system, developed over more than 70 years of its existence, combined with the elements of the new, created substantial confusion about the best way forward. The real choice was in any case limited: either to go back through repression to the old-style Soviet system, which still represented in the eyes of millions of Russians the lost security, non-conflict and paternalistic state attitudes or to advance fully to the creation of a market economy with its complementary phenomena of unemployment, inflation and the long forgotten need to rely on one's own strengths and abilities.

After an initial push democratization and *glasnost* created their own logical development which, as events demonstrated, became uncontrollable, and which represented the death knell of not only the former communist system of politics and economy, but the country itself. By the early 1990s the communists were speedily losing power. The failed coup of 1991 discredited the Communist Party completely. The loss of its coercive powers brought about the dissolution of the Soviet Union. Russia was now facing a situation where 'neither state bureaucracy nor market performed coordination functions in the economy' (Ernst *et al.*, 1996:214). By 1992, when the economic reform package was introduced, Russian industry was experiencing perhaps the most difficult period since the revolution of 1917.

A shock therapy reform package was introduced in Russia in 1992 under the presidency of Gorbachev's successor, Yeltsin. According to Kotz with Weir (1997), the major points of the shock therapy reform package and its results were as follows. Minimum government involvement and maximum speed were the slogans of the reformers. The economic policy based on the shock therapy concept included the following elements: price liberalization; complete elimination of all elements and policies of resource allocation; privatization of state assets (enterprises and land); macroeconomic stabilization (a balanced budget to be achieved by means of a reduction of government spending together with a tight monetary policy); opening up of the economy to international trade and foreign direct investment.

Price liberalization, or in other words elimination of state control over prices, was intended to make prices, determined now by the interaction of supply and demand, perform the function of signalling to companies what to produce and how to produce it at minimum cost, i.e., liberalized prices would reflect what consumers really wanted. The policy of macroeconomic stabilization was devised to slow down and then eliminate inflation. All public sector pro-grammes, subsidies to enterprises and military spending were severely curtailed. These measures were accompanied by sharp Central Bank actions to reduce the money supply and growth of credit.

Rapid mass privatization radically changed the economic foundations of Russian society, turning state property into private property. It was obvious to the reformers that such a colossal task could not be accomplished overnight, especially in the case of large state enterprises. However, intermediate measures, such as conversion into joint-stock companies with the state as majority share-holder, were foreseen. It was intended that at a later date shares would be trans-ferred to private shareholders.

The remaining mechanisms of the formerly mighty centrally planned economy were to be wiped out completely. The measures to achieve this included abolition of all governmental orders which required enterprises to produce a certain volume of output for the state. Only the military indus-trial complex was excluded from this latter measure. From now on market forces were the 'sole mechanism of coordination for the economy' (Kotz with Weir, 1997:163). Free trade and free inflow and outflow of capital were the final items in the reformers' package. Import and export restrictions were to be eliminated both on foreign investment in Russia and on Russian investment abroad.

Shock therapy was intended to replace the old Soviet system as quickly as possible without using 'parts of the old system to help to construct the new one' (ibid.). The results of such revolutionary measures on Russian society and economy are extremely complex and contain many contradictions. Since 1990 Russia has experienced substantial economic decline, as measured by a range of indicators. Output has plummeted across the traditional sectors of industry, agriculture and construction. Compared to 1990, the output of these sectors in 1998 was only 46, 58 and 31 per cent respectively. In terms of GDP services is now the leading sector. The population of private companies, moreover, had by 1997 expanded enormously and accounted for 73 per cent of GDP, even though employing only just under 40 per cent of the total labour force. There had also been a steep rise in official unemployment which exceeded 11 per cent by 1997. Not surprisingly, real wages have on average tended to decline (*Wirtschaftslage und Reformprozesse in Mittel- und Osteuropa*, 1999:193).

It has been argued that the decline is not so dramatic as portrayed by official statistics and that substantial economic activity remains unrecorded, because individual operators can benefit from tax evasion. Companies too can lessen their tax burdens by underreporting performance measures such as revenue. However, Russia does not appear to offer attractive opportunities to foreign investors. In the period 1989–97 cumulative FDI per capita was only US$ 64, a figure considerably lower than for any of the other countries of CEE supported by the European Bank for Reconstruction and Development (EBRD), apart from Macedonia. In 1997 alone the annual figure per head came to no more than US$ 24, less than Bulgaria and Romania, albeit higher than the Ukraine and Belarus (EBRD, 1998:17). All in all the circumstances and prospects of the Russian economy appear bleak.

Companies and managers

The establishment of the market economy has had a considerable impact on companies and their managers. Before 1992 the state was the key institution for economic decision making. From that date on managers had to act on their own initiative in order to secure the continuing existence of their enterprises. One manager of an enterprise in Volgograd commented: 'Before (the reforms) the state was like a good and forgiving mother and not really a very demanding mother. Now the state acts as if the only thing it is interested in are taxes and taxes and nothing else. Its policy actually adds to our problems' (Edwards *et al.*, 2000:140).

The far reaching consequences of the reforms for companies are evidenced by the results of a questionnaire survey of managers in Volgograd conducted in 1997 (Edwards *et al.*, 2000).

Substantial changes had taken place in enterprise structures. The role and activity of planning, production and R&D departments had declined, with increasing importance being attached to accounting, finance, marketing and logistics. The structure of enterprises had become simpler and more transparent. The implementation of new structures was, however, hampered by a reliance on hierarchical flows of communication and the difficulty of finding employees to fill newly created roles in areas such as marketing.

At the same time the role of the trades unions and other 'informal' structures had weakened. Many enterprises no longer provided employees with social benefits such as housing and recreational facilities. Trades unions were now so weak that they could not even guarantee the payment of employees' wages – which in reality were often paid with considerable delay or in the form of goods.

Because of the reforms and the worsening economic circumstances enterprises had closed or had shed a large number of employees. In many instances, however, the reduction of the labour force was proportionately less than the fall in output. Whilst resourceful individuals would frequently leave ailing enterprises in order to seek more secure or more rewarding employment, there was also a great reluctance on the part of managers to fire employees. One human resources manager stated: 'It was very difficult to get used to the idea of saying goodbye to people. It took two to three years to understand that the enterprise just cannot survive without cuts. Some people were hysterical. We did not have any experience at all how to handle the redundancies' (Edwards *et al.*, 2000:75).

A major problem facing companies was mutual indebtedness which had increased enormously since the market reforms. Companies were as a consequence relying to a great extent on barter and promissory notes. Financial issues were therefore a priority area and the role of finance departments had become critical and had changed enormously. Previously such departments had merely produced reports of the current situation. Now finance departments were actively involved in accounting and financial management, seeking out sources of finance, pressurizing debtors and identifying new ways of clearing mutual debts and credits. One manager described the finance department as 'the heart of the enterprise' on which the company depended for its well-being (Edwards *et al.*, 2000:142).

More broadly, companies are exploring a number of strategies to improve their liquidity. These include finding new markets, increasing the efficiency of management and production, analysing demand more effectively, raising product quality, finding cash buyers and becoming more involved in retailing (where goods are sold only for cash).

The new managerial elite

One outcome of the economic reforms launched in 1992 was the widespread transfer of state assets into private hands. A large proportion of former state assets was 'appropriated' by enterprise directors and managers, with insider ownership the dominant form of corporate governance. The entire privatization process has been accompanied by considerable 'controversy and scandal' and economic power in Russia is largely held by a small group of so-called 'oligarchs'. The 'oligarchs' 'are opposed to any reforms that would introduce more transparency in the operation of the economy' (Lavigne, 1999:185).

Furthermore, many privatizations have not complied with the stipulations of the 1991 Law on Privatization and are consequently technically illegal. Bim (1996:473) has observed that: 'The main distinction between Russian insider ownership and the classical model of collective ownership is the absolutely predominant role of managers in governance and control over Russian privatized enterprises that are formally owned by all categories of insiders'.

It is not unusual for enterprise management to do everything possible to prevent outsiders gaining an interest in the enterprise, even if this involvement could benefit the enterprise. A typical example of such behaviour was reported in *Argumenty i Fakty* (1998/48). American investors expressed an interest in investing in a textile factory. One of their conditions was that they should acquire a majority of the company's assets. The enterprise director reacted by appealing to the patriotic feelings of the workforce, using such phrases as 'Americans are buying up our Motherland' and 'You will all be on the streets and American robots will do the jobs'. Such appeals were successful and, in spite of the obvious benefits of foreign investment for the company's future, American involvement was turned down by the workforce.

Managers, particularly senior managers, have without doubt been the main beneficiaries of the privatization and transformation of the Russian economy. Middle managers have benefited from the decline and/or disappearance of external bodies such as the industrial ministry, Communist Party and trades union. They now wield substantial and effective power over the workforce as well as participating in the benefits of enhanced salaries and possibly of a share of ownership of the company. Only those middle managers who are not able to perform satisfactorily under the new circumstances may be in danger of losing their positions.

Senior managers similarly enjoy many of the benefits of increased power, however, to a far greater degree. Many senior managers act and behave as owners of the enterprise (which in many cases they are). Many have acquired a substantial proportion of the company's shares. Ownership and control of the enterprise provide senior managers with a golden opportunity to demonstrate their expertise, earn high salaries and become wealthy. As in a majority of cases external shareholders are in no position to wield a significant degree of power, the power of senior managers may appear and sometimes is absolute.

Polonsky and Iviozian (1999) have argued that enterprise owners and company managers are, in addition to banks and financial groups, trade unions, regional administrations and criminal groups, often opposed to enterprise restructuring which is detrimental to their respective special interests. Restructuring is often doomed to fail because stakeholders are concerned primarily with their own short-term interests rather than acting as strategic investors seeking to achieve long-term goals. Such short-term behaviour is tolerated, even fostered, by an environment marked by corruption and criminality.

According to Polonsky and Iviozian (1999:275), 'the only group, which is truly interested in the restructuring of the enterprise, is the group of middle managers'. The reasons for this are that middle managers are in general competent. Many middle managers were educated and began their working lives after the launch of *perestroika*. Consequently they have been less 'deformed' by the practices of the former economic system. As they are often excluded from participating in the benefits of the enterprise's undeclared activities, they have no interest in supporting such practices and maintaining the status quo. They are also able to work flexibly and innovatively in dealing with the enterprise's problems. 'There is only one drawback, though: they are the least influential people at the enterprise. They do not have the power of workers and top managers and they are least organized' (Polonsky and Iviozian, 1999:275).

A typology of Russian managers

Rogovsky *et al.* (1997) have developed a typology of Russian managers. It is not surprising that in view of the rapid transition from a command to a market economy and the current circumstances of great uncertainty and instability the typology contains a majority of what may be regarded as negative types.

The first type is the socialist manager, comprising those managers who continue to behave according to the codes of practice of the former system. Such managers are characterized by an absence of initiative. They are inclined to avoid uncertainty by refusing to deviate from established practices, relying extensively on bureaucratic procedures. Following procedures is, however, not the same as actually carrying out the procedures and such behaviour is frequently unproductive (Hickson and Pugh, 1995:139–40).

The second type are so-called pragmatic managers. These managers have a predominantly technocratic approach to business issues, for example, concerning themselves more with products than with markets. Their way of thinking is on the whole short term.

The third type are described as predatory managers. They are driven by a desire for success and self-interest. They aim to eliminate competitors and are not averse to cheating on partners, customers and the state authorities. Their perspective is predominantly short term although they are clearly capable of demonstrating considerable initiative.

The fourth group are regarded as socially responsible managers. These managers 'link business performance to the promotion of social and national interests, the resolution of social problems, and universal human values and beliefs' (Rogovsky *et al.*, 1997:8).

In a survey conducted in Moscow in 1993 less than one third of managers surveyed reported that they valued caring more than assertiveness. Under one half admitted to having a future orientation in their business activities and under one third demonstrated an inclination to display initiative (Rogovsky *et al.*, 1997:9). The predominant group tended to be predatory managers.

What distinguished socially responsible managers to a certain degree from the other types was that they were in the 30–45 years age group, had had some experience of the former system, but had not been part of the political establishment, had travelled abroad and had enjoyed an education which had gone beyond the purely technical disciplines.

Maslow (1998) also distinguishes between the values and behaviour of older and younger managers. Older managers have built up their experience under the former system and tend to persist with traditional modes of management. On the other hand, younger managers, who are mainly in middle management positions, desire a greater degree of involvement in decision making and more extensive dialogue with superiors. Maslow has identified relatively little change in managerial values and behaviours in the 1990s and attributes this conservatism in part to managers' technical education. In addition, under the former system, managers had a largely operational role and are thus not accustomed to think and act in a long-term, strategic manner.

Characteristics of Russian managers

The following characterization of Russian managers, particularly senior managers, is derived predominantly from research conducted in Volgograd in southeast Russia (Edwards *et al.*, 2000). In many ways the description may be considered as more generally typical of Russian managers than research conducted in Moscow and St Petersburg, cities which have been more open to western influence, having attracted an overwhelming proportion of foreign direct investment.

Russian society has historically displayed strong collective characteristics. Smith (1976:375) noted 'a kind of primeval sense of community'. Communism reinforced (and to a degree perverted) this sense of community by subordinating the individual (and individual desires and aspirations) to the needs of society and the Party. However, collectivism predates communism. The novelist Vladimir Makanin, referring to events of the mid nineteenth century, records 'the moment when conscience was delegated to the collective, and divine retribution to a group of human beings' (Makanin, 1995:97). According to Maslow (1998:31) a community-based model of economic activity evolved in Russia in the nineteenth century. This model stressed the role of the community rather than the individual, with decisions being taken on a consensual basis. In Maslow's view this community-based model displays a close similarity to economic organization in Asian countries such as Japan, South Korea and Taiwan.

The rapid transition from communism to capitalism has created a situation in which the new economic relationships are neither sufficiently tried nor trusted. New institutions and new commercial practices have yet to establish themselves. There are numerous cases where trust and property have been abused. In such a general context of uncertainty and apprehension, it is not surprising that family members, friends and personal contacts, rather than institutional mechanisms, play a significant role.

Such values and relationships were manifest in Volgograd. The manifestation of these relationships took a number of forms. Firstly, the ownership and management of many enterprises were in the hands of a small group consisting of family members and close friends. Second, family contacts in, for example, the public administration can facilitate access to municipal and provincial resources such as still publicly owned commercial property as well as a certain protection from criminal organizations. In the absence of customary, accepted practices, and the presence of weak institutional forces and powerful criminal tendencies, a reliance on family and friends is clearly a significant economic resource. In the case of barter, to give another example, company directors understandably deal only with intermediaries whom they personally know and trust.

The area of personal trust and contacts expands, however, beyond the circle of close family and friends. What was particularly noticeable in Volgograd was the extensive network of former Communist Party functionaries who were now active in enterprise managements and the public administration. It is not clear whether or what links they have with the current Communist Party. However, they appear to form a local elite encompassing the economic and political spheres.

Personal relationships, both between family members and close friends ('quasi family') and between 'friends' (relationships based on mutual respect, political affiliation or cultural background), involve mutuality and mutual benefit. Favours given have to be repaid if requested. In certain instances this repayment can involve the payment of bribes (monetary or in goods) to the more powerful partner in the relationship.

Clearly such personal relationships have both positive and negative characteristics. On the positive side they permit the conduct of economic transactions in a climate of relative uncertainty, providing reliable information and access to trustworthy expertise as well as to other resources. On the negative side such relationships can create new forms of dependency and abuses of political and economic power, increasing corruption and undermining the development of an open market economy. A further manifestation of collectivism is the close relationship between the local economic and political elites. The municipal and provincial administrations have an obvious interest in the activities of the area's major enterprises, especially in the area of employment and social services. Many social functions (e.g. housing, health, pre-school education) are being abandoned by companies and are becoming the concern of the public administration even if there are few or no resources to carry them out. Part of the problem of local administrations is that the relationships between the various levels of government (federal, regional, provincial and municipal) are firstly not always clear and secondly a source of conflict.

However, the respective degree of power of business and local political leaders has been reversed, with many companies now in a strong position to dictate to the local administration. One company interviewee described the changing relationship in the following way: 'Before the reforms we (enterprise and local authorities) were like in a marriage without love: suspicious of each other, forced to care for each other in formal relations established by Party Committees. Now we are free and the relations which we have are our own. We are partners with local administrations, sharing the same objectives: keep people in employment, try paying them for what they have earned, get the plant right because healthy enterprises mean healthier local finances' (Edwards *et al.*, 2000: 148). Not surprisingly, local politicians may take a different view. A director of a large industrial enterprise in a city close to Volgograd was approached by the local mayor who asked him to donate a considerable sum of money. On refusing, the director heard the mayor utter bitterly: 'You would have been stripped of your Communist Party membership if you had answered like that in the past' (*Press Klub*, 1997/11: 3).

Political power in itself can moreover be attractive to people in business. Previously there was a certain interchangeability between positions in the political (both party and administrative) and the economic spheres. This still applies to a certain degree today, as senior members of the local administration and deputies of the Duma may come from senior positions in economic organizations. Some company directors may also see political office as a way of extending their economic power, by increasing their range of contacts and gaining privileged access to public contracts and finance. One company director claimed to have recouped the costs of his electoral campaign in only three days as a member of the provincial parliament.

Although the research by Rogovsky *et al.* (1997) indicated a widespread lack of initiative among Russian managers, in the new political and economic climate entrepreneurship has mushroomed and has taken a variety of forms and nuances. For example, retailing has been transformed from a bleak state-controlled system prone to endemic shortages to a dynamic, if somewhat variable, constellation of innumerable providers of goods and services. The general transformation created an opportunity for individuals to engage in trading and retail activities; many individuals gladly seized this opportunity; many were pushed through necessity because of unemployment or general financial constraint.

Managers of formerly state-owned enterprises too could no longer adhere to the economic practices of the past and had to become opportunity-seekers, if their enterprises were to undergo a satisfactory transformation and survive. The new entrepreneurial activities can be classified as either legal, illegal or criminal. Legal activity comprises individuals who operate openly and account for their income to the relevant state bodies such as the tax authorities. There is also small-scale illegal activity such as operating an unregistered taxi service and carrying out relatively small jobs for cash. The definition becomes somewhat more problematical when applied to the 'piggy-back' entrepreneurial activities which operate within existing and, in some cases, even within defunct enterprises and involve collusion between enterprise managements and the operators of the activity. Clearly such activities, which are intended to defraud the tax authorities, make illicit use of company property by not reimbursing the company for the use of its physical and energy resources and enrich personally the individuals involved, are a long way removed from those of the unlicensed taxi driver who is generally acting solely in order to earn a living for himself and his family.

Substantial entrepreneurism is also evident in relation to the current political structures at all levels (Malle, 1996; Skuratov, 1998). The directors of former state enterprises have maintained and cultivated their relationships with federal and local politicians in order to obtain state funding and other support. As already noted, even directors of new private companies believe that economic benefits can be derived from personal involvement in political activities.

Regrettably, all too often this interaction with the political authorities degenerates into bribery and corruption, both for large and small firms. Furthermore, this kind of 'entrepreneurial' activity is resource-consuming with regard to both time and money and represents in a narrow economic sense a poor use of the company's resources. To make matters worse, particularly for smaller companies, managements also have to respond to the attentions of criminal organizations extracting payment for the 'roof' or protection money.

The interaction with political bodies can also be interpreted as an attempt to resist the development of competitive markets. There appears to be a desire to recreate monopolies, even in the more competitive markets. This desire expresses itself in anti-competitive behaviour (e.g. restricting supplies) and in vertical integration (e.g. expansion into retailing and special contractual and other relationships with suppliers). Once again, this conduct is understandable in the context of the current economic situation and the recent history of company managements. It is almost as if they wish to recreate the certainties of the former economic system, by controlling suppliers and customers, and creating a monopolistic barrier against competitors. While these aspirations are understandable at the level of individual firms, they are furthermore in no way discouraged by the institutional context in which they operate.

Organizational management

The internal management of organizations is generally characterized by traditional autocratic and hierarchical relationships and by a general climate of paternalism. Organizations continue to be structured in a largely hierarchical fashion, with vertical lines of communication. Some of the managers interviewed in Volgograd commented that there was a clear need for more effective communication across functional areas as well as for greater informal interaction. One manager noted: 'We still do not communicate well with each other. We are good at receiving orders and passing them further down, but we do not know how to talk about our common tasks to our colleagues in the parallel structures' (Edwards *et al.*, 2000:139).

The problem of communication appeared to be exacerbated by the autocratic behaviour of managers and of owner-managers in particular. The traditional autocratic style of management, based on superiors issuing orders and subordinates carrying out instructions, had been reinforced by the unwillingness of individuals to assume personal responsibility and the weakness of employee

organizations. These aspects are reinforced when senior managers are synonymous with company owners. What seems to have developed in many enterprises
is a kind of paternalism where employees look to the managing director to safe-
guard their interests and the senior management team continues to express a
genuine responsibility towards the body of employees. This paternalism is exemplified by the experience of enterprise demanning where job cuts, even when
massive, are proportionately less than might have been expected, taking into
account the actual decline in sales volume. Any cuts that are made thus appear
to have been 'forced' upon senior management.

Management learning

Managers have experienced substantial changes since the 'shock therapy'
reforms of 1992. Companies have become autonomous entities operating in a
more or less free market. As a consequence managers have had to implement
policies of survival and restructuring. Previously neglected functions such as
marketing and human resource management have come to the forefront as companies need to market their products, raise the productivity of the workforce
and even make individuals redundant.

A key concern of managers has been to raise the quality of production, by
reducing wastage and improving process and product quality. One Volgograd
company established a quality control division. The company was seeking to
achieve ISO 9000 certification. New quality control mechanisms have been
introduced, leading to a reduction in customer complaints. Quality circles have
also been introduced and substantial training of managers and shopfloor
workers is an integral part of the development process.

Another Volgograd company, following the unexpectedly costly execution of
an overseas order, likewise applied for ISO 9000 certification, with the overall
aim of upgrading the quality of products, the production process and of reducing costs. In so doing, the company was collaborating with a number of research
institutes. In order to disseminate new knowledge and techniques internally the
company had set up its own training centre where it ran courses for employees
to increase their commercial and technical expertise.

The demands on managers had changed completely from the past. In the past
they had merely carried out orders. Now they had to be proactive and knowl-
edgeable and professionalism, rather than party affiliation, was considered
essential. One manager in Volgograd described key managerial characteristics
in the following way: mobility, romanticism, devotion, energy and a calculat-
ing mind.

Managers stressed in particular the need to be appropriately qualified. Some
top managers were trying to raise their own level of expertise by, for example,

attending courses at a regional quality centre. Many companies, however, lack the financial resources to provide training.

Managers now clearly exercised greater power than in the past. Many managers commented on the need to become better qualified and more experienced and to update their knowledge continuously, in spite of pressures of time. Managers also needed to assume greater responsibility for training the future generation of managers.

Managers believed they had more (some said much more) power. Managerial power was considered not to have been given, but taken and such power led to profit. One interviewee in Volgograd commented on the self-interest of managers, many of whom appear concerned only by their own high salaries. As another manager exclaimed: 'They've got everything!' (Edwards *et al.*, 2000:153).

The change in the system of economic management has had a particularly dramatic impact on the position and behaviour of managers in Russia. This impact has been accentuated by the sheer size of the country and by the psychological repercussions of the collapse of an ideology of which Russia had been the leading exponent and practitioner. Furthermore, the process of establishing new state institutions has been slow and has encountered numerous difficulties. In this context enterprise directors and senior managers have been able to assume positions providing considerable power and, in many instances, considerable personal wealth.

References

Argumenty i Fakty, St. Petersburg, weekly.

Arnason, J. (1993) *The Future that Failed, Origins and Destinies of the Soviet Model*, London: Routledge.

Bim, A. (1996) 'Ownership and Control of Enterprises', *Communist Economies and Economic Transformation*, 8/4, pp. 471–500.

Dyker, A. (1992) *Restructuring the Soviet Economy*, London: Routledge.

EBRD (1998) *Annual Report 1997*, London: EBRD.

Edwards, V., Polonsky, G. and Polonsky, A. (2000) *The Russian Province after Communism, Enterprise Continuity and Change*, Basingstoke and London: Macmillan.

Ernst, M., Alexeev, M. and Marer, P. (1996) *Transforming the Core*, Boulder, Colorado: Westview Press.

Gaddy, C. (1996) *The Price of the Past*, Washington, D.C.: Brookings Institution Press.

Granick, D. (1960) *The Red Executive, A Study of the Organization Man in Russian Industry*, London: Macmillan.

Hickson, D. and Pugh, D. (1995) *Management Worldwide, The Impact of Societal Culture on Organizations around the Globe*, Harmondsworth: Penguin.

Kotkin, S. (1995) *Magnetic Mountain, Stalinism as a Civilization*, Berkeley: University of California Press.

Kotz, D. with Weir, F. (1997) *The Revolution from Above*, London: Routledge.

Lavigne, M. (1999) *The Economics of Transition, From Socialist Economy to Market Economy*, Basingstoke and London: Macmillan, 2nd ed.

Makanin, V. (1995) *Baize-covered Table with Decanter*, London: Readers International.

Malle, S (1996) 'Russian Entrepreneurship and Business in Transition: Towards the Re-building of State Conglomerates', *Journal of International and Comparative Economics*, 20, pp. 37–64.

Maslow, W. (1998) 'Wertorientierungen und Stereotype beim Führungsverhalten von Managern in Russland', in Lang, R. (ed.), *Führungskräfte im osteuropäischen Transformationsprozeß*, III. Chemnitzer Ostforum, Munich and Mering: Rainer Hampp, pp. 27–35.

Polonsky, G. and Iviozian, Z. (1999) 'Restructuring of Russian Industries – is it Really Possible?', in Edwards V. (ed.), Proceedings of the Fifth Annual Conference on *The Impact of Transformation on Individuals, Organizations, Society*, Chalfont St. Giles: CREEB, vol. 1, pp. 267–77.

Press Klub, Volgograd, irregular.

Rogovsky, N., Grachev, M. and Bertocchi, S. (1997) 'Social Exclusion and Business Initiatives in the Economies in Transition: The Case of Russia', *New Partnership for Social Cohesion Working Paper Series No. 6*, Copenhagen: The Danish National Institute of Social Research (Socialforskningsinstituttet).

Skuratov, Y. (1998) 'La corruzione nella Russia di oggi e le vie per sconfiggerla', in *La criminalità transnazionale organizzata, Dal riciclaggio all'usura*, Turin: Società Editrice Internazionale, pp. 91–101.

Smith, H. (1976) *The Russians*, London: Sphere.

Wirtschaftslage und Reformprozesse in Mittel- und Osteuropa (1999), Berlin: Bundesministerium für Wirtschaft und Technologie.

CHAPTER 5

Czech and Slovak management

At the end of the Second World War in 1945 the former Czechoslovakia had proportionately one of the largest communist parties in Europe. A distinctive feature of postwar Czechoslovak history has been the attempt of communists in the former Czechoslovakia to create a form of democratic communism, a process culminating in the Prague Spring of 1968. The crushing of the Prague Spring in 1969 by the armed forces of the Soviet Union and various other Warsaw Pact countries resulted in the widespread rejection of communism by the Czechoslovaks.

A further distinguishing feature since 1989 has been the impact of centrifugal forces on the country, culminating in the so-called 'Velvet Divorce'. Since 1993 the Czech and Slovak Republics have been independent states. The 'Velvet Divorce' has tended to emphasize the differences between the two countries and in fact the experience of a unified Czechoslovak state has been relatively brief, lasting only for the periods 1918–1939 and 1945–1992. Nearly two thirds of this period was spent under communism.

In order to identify both the similarities and differences between Czech and Slovak management it has been decided to focus initially on Czech management and only subsequently to extend the discussion to management in Slovakia.

Following the Second World War Czechoslovakia found itself behind the Iron Curtain, even though the westernmost part of the country had actually been liberated by the western allies. Czechoslovakia was in a number of ways very different from the vast majority of countries which had come under the influence of the Soviet Union. These differences were of both an economic and socio-political nature.

Economically, Czechoslovakia (especially the so-called Czech lands of Bohemia and Moravia) had been a leading industrial power before 1939. Industry, especially light industry, had developed during the nineteenth century when Bohemia and Moravia had been part of the Habsburg Empire. The two provinces were in many respects the economic powerhouse of the Empire, producing around 70 per cent of its total industrial output, specializing in light engineering activities (Zauberman, 1976). Only East Germany within COMECON could boast of a similar scale of industrialization.

Politically too, Czechoslovakia was different from the other states in CEE. Firstly, Czechoslovakia prided itself on its democratic traditions and secondly (once again East Germany apart) it had one of the largest indigenous Communist Parties in Europe. In the 1946 elections the Czechoslovak Communist Party gained 38 per cent of the votes in what has been regarded as relatively free elections. Czechoslovakia thus offered the Soviet Union a strong economic base (a positive factor) and a strong democratic tradition and civic culture (a negative factor from the Soviet point of view).

However, these distinguishing features did not apply equally to both the Czech and Slovak parts of the country. Slovakia's industrial development lagged far behind that of Bohemia and Moravia. The Second World War, moreover, had divided Czechs and Slovaks. The Czech lands, minus the predominantly German-speaking areas of the Sudetenland which had been incorporated directly into the German Reich, became a German protectorate. Slovakia on the other hand became a separate state dependent on Nazi Germany. The 'Velvet Divorce' of 1993 consequently evolved out of the tensions inherent in the Czecho-Slovak relationship which had in 1918 brought together two parts of the former Austro-Hungarian Empire each of which had its own view of its historical development. At this point we will turn to factors which have moulded the Czech national identity, returning later to the situation in Slovakia.

National identity

The key turning point in Czech history was the Battle of the White Mountain (Bila Hora) in 1620. Prior to this date Prague had been the capital of a substantial empire founded in the early tenth century and a significant cultural centre in Central Europe. The Charles University had been founded in Prague in 1348. Following the defeat of the Czech armies at the Battle of the White Mountain the Czech lands lost their independence and were dominated by foreign rulers, for most of the period up to 1918 by the Habsburgs in Vienna. In the fourteenth century the spirit of the Reformation swept through the Czech lands, finding widespread support. The election of a Catholic Habsburg to the Bohemian throne in 1526 did not find favour with Czech protestants and the country was frequently in turmoil. A rebellion in 1618 was crushed at the White Mountain. The Czech protestants (or Hussites, that is, followers of Jan Hus) were forced to recant or flee the country when the Counter-Reformation (driven to a considerable degree by the Habsburgs) was victorious. Most Czechs accordingly readopted Catholicism, which became the state religion in 1627.

The period of Habsburg domination following the conclusion of the Counter-Reformation was characterized by the imposition of rule from Vienna, the surveilling presence of the Habsburg bureaucracy and steady Germanization of Czech life and culture, which was particularly noticeable in Prague and other urban centres. German became the official language of instruction in 1774.

The nineteenth century, however, witnessed a revival of Czech language, cultural life and national identity. The nineteenth century was after all a century of nationalistic aspirations throughout Europe. These developments went hand in hand with the emergence of Bohemia and Moravia as areas of significant industrialization. The growth of industry in the urban centres encouraged emigration from the still largely Czech rural areas and helped Czech culture to reassert itself in Prague and other towns. Industrialization and economic growth also gave rise to a Czech middle class oriented to industrial and commercial activities. This situation was in clear contrast to other CEE countries where such a group failed to develop or consisted mainly of foreign entrepreneurs.

The establishment of an independent state in 1918 was very much the fulfilment of Czech aspirations. However, the new state was not solely Czechoslovak. Czechs were barely 50 per cent of the total population, Czechs and Slovaks combined around two thirds. Czechoslovakia in fact had more Germans (over 3 millions) than Slovaks as well as substantial minorities of Hungarians and Ukrainians (Wiskemann, 1966:267). There were moreover tensions between the various national groups, even between Czechs and Slovaks. The most bitter dispute, however, was between Czechs and Germans. This dispute became particularly virulent with the rise of Nazism in Germany. Pressure from Germany and the policy of appeasement espoused by Britain and France led to the Munich Agreement of 1938 by which Czechoslovakia transferred territories with a Germany majority to Nazi Germany.

In spite of these difficulties Czechoslovakia was one of the most democratic and liberal states in CEE and its economic structure withstood the Depression of the inter-war years particularly well. During the period of German occupation (1939–45) there was an expansion of heavy industry, driven by the needs of the German military.

In 1945 Czechoslovakia became part of the Soviet sphere of influence. Many people had felt deceived and betrayed by the outcome of appeasement and welcomed closer relations with the Soviet Union whose forces had liberated the main part of the country. The mass expulsion of the Sudetenland Germans had Soviet support and many saw the Soviet Union as a guarantor of Czechoslovakia's independence if there were any future threat of German aggression. The new post-war government also introduced social democratic policies such as nationalization of industrial concerns and banks. The communists were major partners in the government coalition and enjoyed considerable popular support (as well as holding strategic areas of power and control such as the army and police force).

In 1948 the Communist Party seized total control of the state and established a communist regime on the Soviet model. From 1948 to 1989 – excluding the Prague Spring of 1968–69 – Czechoslovakia was one of the closest imitators of the Soviet model. Central planning was introduced; priority was given to heavy industry; the industrial landscape became dominated by large conglomerates; and private ownership of the means of production was virtually eliminated. By 1952, 98 per cent of industrial assets had been nationalized (Clark and Soulsby, 1999:55).

The Czechoslovak communists, however, comprised one of the strongest Stalinist elements in the CEE communist parties (Arnason, 1993:152). This Stalinism manifested itself in the show trials of the 1950s which were directed even against leading members of the Party. The Prague Spring of 1968–69, when reformers took over control of the Communist Party and sought to establish a 'socialism with a human face', had the aim of transforming the economic and political spheres. Although winning widespread popular support, the proposed reforms aroused the enmity of conservative elements within the Czechoslovak Party as well as in the leaderships of the Soviet Union and several other CEE countries. The Prague Spring ended with the invasion of Czechoslovakia in 1969 when military forces of the Soviet Union and other CEE countries occupied Czechoslovakia. There followed a period of intense repression in which supporters of the reforms were expelled from the Party and were removed from positions of authority (this included managerial positions). The last 20 years of the communist regime in Czechoslovakia proved a dour experience for the majority of the population, with the regime demonstrating a considerable degree of inflexibility, especially when compared to the situation in Hungary and Poland. The regime finally collapsed in 1989 – other communist regimes had already toppled and there was considerable popular pressure for change. The 'Velvet Revolution' ensured that change came largely peacefully.

National characteristics

The periods of Habsburg domination (1526–1918), German occupation (1939–1945) and the communist regime (1948–1989) developed and reinforced a number of national characteristics. Czechs portray themselves as peaceful and anti-militaristic, the victims of other countries' aggression. Allied to this is a tradition of quiet resistance. This resistance may appear passive but the Czechs, according to the Nazi Reichsprotektor Reinhard Heydrich,* 'were spineless flexible twigs that bent down under pressure, only to lash back when least

---

* Heydrich was assassinated in 1942 by the Czech resistance after having let his guard slip (Foot, M. [1976] *Resistance*, London: Paladin/Granada Publishing, pp. 205–206).

expected' (Kuras, 1996:15). This tradition of generally passive resistance may, however, degenerate into an abdication of any responsibility for one's own actions. The Czechs, moreover, consider themselves to be unique and self-sufficient. During the Habsburg period Czechs consistently asserted their own identity against that of their Austrian rulers. The outcome of appeasement and the German occupation proved to a considerable extent that the Czechs could rely only on themselves. This feeling of self-sufficiency can deteriorate into an antipathy for anything that is not Czech.

The long periods of foreign domination and oppression also assisted the development of a social consensus. The revival of Czech identity and culture in the nineteenth century involved all social classes, and this social consensus was on the whole reinforced by the experience of German occupation and communism.

These characteristics also translate into the economic sphere and workplace in a number of guises. There is confidence in a Czech approach to management and a feeling that there is little or nothing to be learned from expertise and practice in other countries. Such sentiment can often turn into a disdain for foreign 'experts' and investors. Passive resistance moreover was a feature of working life after 1969 when 'workers pretended to work and enterprises pretended to pay them' (a frequently quoted maxim).

Czech management

Unlike the majority of countries in CEE, the Czechs are able to boast of an industrial and capitalist tradition going back to the middle of the nineteenth century. Three main strands can be identified in this tradition: autocracy, a technical bias and paternalism. Czech industrialists and their managers were typically autocratic individuals. This autocracy, however, was balanced by a concern for the welfare of the company's employees. Furthermore, technical knowledge and skills were regarded as the necessary foundation for managerial practice. Forms of scientific management such as Taylorism and Fordism were much appreciated and implemented.

An example of the Czech system of management, possibly in its most idealistic form, is portrayed in the development and growth of the Bata company. Bata grew in the early part of the twentieth century into one of the world's largest shoe manufacturers. The Bata management system (Bata, 1992; Zeleny, 1993) was derived from Fordism, but also focused on employees as shareholders in the company. The Bata management system provided education and training for the employees and the company's influence extended into the town in which it was based and was the main employer. Bata was also involved in the political administration of its local community. The local administration was dominated by the Bata Party, with Tomas Bata, the company's founder, as mayor.

The Czech manager under socialism

The prerequisite for being a manager under the communist regime was generally an engineering qualification and party membership. The management style was strongly hierarchical and autocratic. The hierarchical nature of decision making was reinforced by the overall industrial organization, with its preponderance of large conglomerates which reduced the autonomy of individual enterprises. The authoritarian approach in management style was paralleled by the authoritarianism and rigidity of the political system. As in other command economies, managers were driven by the need to achieve production targets:

> It was in the interests of managers at all levels to do all they could to ensure the visible attainment of production targets. Those managers of units which demonstrably failed to realize plans were liable to be demoted, moved or otherwise to lose status and access to associated 'privileges' (e.g. cars, foreign travel, special accommodation) (Clark and Soulsby, 1999:65).

The extensive nature of hierarchical relationships and the fear of punishment (Clark and Soulsby, 1999:80) appear to be particularly distinguishing features of the communist system of management in Czechoslovakia. This hard-line managerial style also went hand in hand with a degree of paternalism, especially as it regarded relationships with the local community. Enterprises were directly responsible for providing many social services such as housing as well as recreational facilities. The links between enterprise and community were particularly strong where the enterprise was the main employer in a relatively small community. The links moreover were not purely institutional links but links between individuals. Managers and workers and their respective families tended to know each other on a personal basis. If one adds to this the tendency for managers to work in the locality where they originated and managerial mobility was considerably limited, strong interpersonal ties tended to develop. At a more senior managerial level such personal ties would extend beyond the local community into the regional and national structures of power. Nevertheless, the influence of the local community was especially significant and senior managers would be accorded recognition for the benefits they brought to the enterprise and consequently to the local community.

The period of so-called 'normalization' after the crushing of the Prague Spring in 1969 had a direct impact on enterprise management. Firstly those managers who had supported the Prague Spring were demoted and/or transferred. Secondly, their positions were taken by managers who were either insufficiently qualified and/or were regarded as 'illegitimate' by the majority of the workforce (Clark and Soulsby, 1999). The 'normalization' process in fact widened the gap between the rulers and the ruled. Opponents of normalization withdrew into a private world. In the workplace this withdrawal took the form of a passive resistance to the system, to pretending to work. Managers were thus faced with an increasingly demotivated and demoralized workforce, for whom the managerial group lacked any kind of legitimacy. This situation heightened the tension between appearances and reality, between how the system was supposed to operate and the way it actually functioned. Managers were thus forced to conceal the ever increasing gap between planning targets and actual outcomes. According to Clark and Soulsby (1999:103):

> The social reality simply reinforced managers' interests in making the system *look as if it were working*: for example, by exploiting state socialist processes like soft budgeting to renegotiate targets, or by distorting the production information to create the appearance of plan fulfilment.

Right up to 1989 and the Velvet Revolution Czechoslovakia remained one of the most tightly controlled and authoritarian regimes in CEE. It had also been one of the countries which, the Prague Spring apart, had done the least to create a more flexible and responsive economic structure. In spite of these factors and the issue of the legitimacy of the regime and, within enterprises, of managers, the Czechoslovak economy was in many respects more sound than that of many of its COMECON neighbours. Throughout the communist period Czechoslovak enterprises had enjoyed a degree of export success and, in comparison to other COMECON countries, had accumulated only a relatively small external debt. Furthermore, the country's pre-war economic and democratic legacy placed it possibly on a more favourable footing than most of the other countries in CEE.

After communism

The new democratic regime that came to power in 1989 embarked on a policy of rapid market liberalization and privatization, one of whose aims was to destroy the influence of the former political elite, including managers regarded as instruments of the former regime. Czechoslovakia's adoption of a 'shock therapy' approach to transformation under finance minister Vaclav Klaus in 1990 was very much a political act, to quote Lavigne (1999:118) 'the expression of the political victory of the conservatives', even though the actual economic conditions were relatively favourable and could have supported a more gradualist approach.

The aim of privatization was to change the economic structure of the economy and to redress the injustices of the former regime. Restitutions to former owners and the privatization of small enterprises were largely completed by 1993. The privatization of large enterprises was more complex and involved a mass voucher scheme whereby individuals were given a certain number of vouchers with which to buy company shares. Many of these vouchers, however, were acquired by banks and private investment funds which consequently became significant shareholders and cross-shareholders (Clark and Soulsby, 1999:132). Compared to other countries in the region there was little evidence of spontaneous or *nomenklatura* privatization (Clark and Soulsby, 1999:128).

Many managers from the old regime, however, felt themselves to be in a position of considerable uncertainty, lacking any professional, personal or social legitimacy. Government attempts to curtail the influence particularly of former communist senior managers resulted in the passing of the so-called Lustration (or Screening) Act which came into effect on 1st January 1992. The aim of the Act was to bar all *nomenklatura* managers from posts in the state-owned sector. The actual effect of the legislation was to encourage such managers either to move into private-sector companies or to expedite the privatization of their own enterprises (Clark and Soulsby, 1999:140). In reality the Screening Act has had only limited impact. According to Clark and Soulsby (1999:226): 'One of the most conspicuous findings of the research has been the degree to which former *nomenklatura* managers have retained positions of power in the privatized enterprises . . .' Ellenbogen (1998) also notes that many old 'sick' companies are still in the hands of apparatchiks who continue to influence attitudes and practices.

The persistence of historical values can also be seen in the attitudes to the involvement of foreign interests in the country. Many of the views on foreign direct investment have been negative and have impeded entry by foreign investors. This has included government intransigence and inconsistency (Mills, 1995:273). Not surprisingly FDI has been limited. This attitude is due in part to the Czech trait of sturdy independence so that 'many managers resent comparison and repeatedly refer to the uniqueness of their conditions . . .' (Hoffmann *et al.*, 1996:2). Foreign advisors and consultants moreover have been the subject of considerable criticism (Mills, 1995:328–330). According to Bygate (1998:250), reporting on interviews with managers in a furniture company, 'The managers complained that western European visitors viewed the Czech Republic as an underdeveloped country and consequently tried to force down the price of products to a level which would not even cover the purchase of raw materials.'

Czech management and the transformation

Considerable changes have taken place in the Czech economy since 1989. The old system of economic management has been swept away. A market economy has been established. The former state-owned enterprises have been at least formally largely privatized. However, the policy of 'shock therapy' has been mitigated by government policies and practices which protect companies and the population from the most extreme effects (Dangerfield, 1997:9). For example, there is evidence that the government has provided tacit support for inefficient enterprises (Clark and Soulsby, 1999:121).

The landscape of enterprises has nevertheless changed substantially. The communist conglomerates have largely been broken up, new firms have emerged including a number of foreign direct investors such as Volkswagen and Nestlé. Many of these 'new' companies, however, have re-established traditional hierarchical structures characterized by top management inflexibility (Maly and Dedina, 1997).

A number of other authors stress the continuity of management attitudes and practices. Rychetnik (1996) notes the tightening of employee discipline as one aspect of an authoritarian management style. Taylorist-Fordist approaches are still predominant, while human resource management continues to be devalued. According to Pavlica and Thorpe (1998) the approach to human resources is still largely technocratic and bureaucratic. The Czech manager is depicted as generally a 'dominant and superior male', a politician who regards non-managers as 'impractical and lazy people' (Pavlica and Thorpe, 1998: 145 and 148). The continuity and authoritarianism/paternalism of Czech management is also reported by Bygate (1998) and Clark and Soulsby (1999), the latter commenting that 'the influential business and management class of the transitional economy comprises largely converted *nomenklatura*' (p. 229).

The inherent critique of the post-1989 evolution of Czech management extends beyond the mere realm of management attitudes and practice and is part of a larger debate concerning the nature of business ethics in the Czech Republic. According to Trick (1999:661):

> Today's 'fin de siècle' Czech Republic is in the midst of a 'velvet' crisis in political, economic and social terms, which in turn infuses the world of Czech business and management. This situation has exposed many cases of corruption and collusion, frequently related to the ownership of (formerly state-owned) enterprises and the use of public funds (often from state-owned banks) to acquire such enterprises and to establish new companies in order to 're-structure' the profitable parts and 'bankrupt' the less desirable elements. Criminal practice, such as intimidation of potential whistle-blowers, is not unknown.

However, it was possibly too much to expect a rapid return to the idealized notion of the inter-war First Republic. Other commentators, moreover, have focused more on areas where there have been visible changes of a positive nature. Hoffmann *et al.* (1996) have developed a typology of Czech managers comprising four archetypes: manager-entrepreneur, manager-professional, manager-passenger and manager-speculator. The authors note that between a quarter and a third of managers gave up their positions after 1989 because of their political past, incompetence or because they had reached retirement age, thus creating openings for new managers. Furthermore, the authors express the view that even older managers are responding to the new operating environment, with professionals and entrepreneurs exerting increasing influence.

Hoffmann *et al.* (1996:4) also give a positive interpretation of aspects of the communist legacy:

> Even in the past system, Czech enterprises worked, some of them with excellent results. Some enterprises were successful exporters to market economies, others were able to develop and implement advanced technologies. The central plan . . . kept creating problems for the enterprise directors . . . Thus, initiative, imagination, perseverance and a certain degree of personal courage were the necessary qualities of a manager.

Mertlik (1996) also identifies some positive aspects of the former system, especially the emergence of more professional managers in the 1980s who began to replace the political appointees made as part of the normalization process after 1969. Mertlik also stresses the enormous volume of managerial learning that has taken place since 1989, with particular improvement in areas such as marketing and R&D. Mertlik (1996), however, identifies continuing areas of weakness such as strategic management and the 'renaissance of what may be termed a type of Taylorist/Fordist corporate culture' (p. 102), although this is regarded as a temporary phenomenon and a consequence of efforts to increase worker discipline.

Savitt (1998) strikes a more cautious note, postulating different degrees of company marketing orientations, depending on whether the company was on the one hand a restructured old enterprise or on the other hand a new or foreign-owned company. Burianek (1997) argues that companies are only gradually absorbing and adopting more modern management principles in areas such as human resource management, an area discredited because of its association with the communist regime's use of cadre and personnel departments to monitor individuals' political reliability. Restructuring that does take place tends to focus on technical and organizational issues rather than external issues impacting on the firm (Mense-Petermann, 1997).

The 'Velvet Divorce'

Czech-Slovak 'frictions' re-emerged after 1989 and were a significant issue of political debate. The differences proved irreconcilable. The Slovaks wanted greater autonomy/independence; the Czechs resented this and considered the

Slovaks as ungrateful (this is clearly a gross oversimplification of a complex debate). The outcome of the differences was that independent Czech and Slovak republics came into being on 1st January 1993. The 'Velvet Divorce' signified the end of a relationship which had existed since 1918. The dissolution of Czechoslovakia also had implications for companies in terms of assets (now located in a foreign country) and of markets, partly as a result of new fiscal and customs arrangements.

Mills (1995:142–145) illustrates the problems for companies by reference to the case of Cokoladovny, the Czech Republic's largest confectionery producer. Cokoladovny suddenly found itself cut off from its Slovak market and 100 Slovak wholesalers. The company was accustomed to supplying each wholesaler directly. However, in consequence of Slovakia's decision to collect VAT locally, necessitating a day's delay because of the formalities, the company was considering establishing one or two warehouses in Slovakia to deal with customs clearance and other procedures and minimize delays. Such an approach, however, was estimated to lead to a 10 per cent increase in distribution costs.

Slovakia

The origins of the differences between Czechs and Slovaks go back almost one thousand years. In the early eleventh century Slovakia became part of Hungary. During the period of the Ottoman occupation of Budapest, the Hungarian capital was transferred to Bratislava (Pozsony in Hungarian). Bratislava/Pozsony was the Hungarian capital for over 200 years (1541–1784). In a similar fashion to the Czech struggle against Germanization, the Slovaks were forced to resist Magyarization in order to retain their own identity. However, much of the ruling Slovak groups did not resist and succumbed to Magyarization. Slovak national identity therefore remained relatively weak, even in the nineteenth century.

Right up to the start of the Second World War Slovakia was a largely agricultural country, with business activities predominantly in the hands of non-Slovaks. The majority of the population was Catholic, as were the Czechs, but there were differences in the respective nationalities' response to religion. The Slovaks tended to be devout Catholics, with the Church playing a pivotal role in everyday life. The Czechs on the other hand were members of a secularized society and generally anti-clerical. The establishment of Czechoslovakia in 1918 had therefore brought together two diverse national groups, with the Czechs dominant in the economic and political spheres. The Slovaks, in contrast, lacked a well developed national identity and civic culture. Furthermore there was considerable resentment of the way the state appeared to favour the Czechs and discriminate against Slovaks.

The annexation of the Sudetenland by Nazi Germany in 1938 highlighted the weaknesses of the Czechoslovak state and in 1939 Slovakia declared its independence under the leadership of Tiso, a Catholic priest. For the period of the Second World War (1939–45) Slovakia remained dependent on German support. According to Wiskemann (1966:177): 'Slovakia, moreover, profited from the Nazi plan of turning it into Hitler's well-dressed shop window to display the joys of living under Nazi protection'.

With the defeat of Nazi Germany in 1945 the Czech and Slovak territories were reunited. In the post-war period the communists brought benefits to Slovakia especially in terms of industrialization, which established heavy industries (for example, armaments, chemicals and steel). In this respect developments in Slovakia followed the more widespread East European model of heavy industrialization whereby a largely agricultural economy was rapidly industrialized and urbanized.

This legacy of communism was to be one of the causes of disagreement between Czech and Slovak politicians after the Velvet Revolution. Because of its particular industrial structure (Slovakia was, for example, home for 60 per cent of the Czechoslovak arms industry), the 'shock therapy' policy launched in 1990 under Finance Minister Klaus was more likely to disadvantage Slovakia than the Czech provinces. This in fact proved to be the case. The fall in output and rise in unemployment hit the Slovaks harder than the Czechs, as the following illustration indicates:

Indicators of Czech and Slovak differences (1994)

	Czech Republic	Slovak Republic
Per capita GDP (US$)	3853	2576
Unemployment (%)	3.2	14.8
Gross industrial output (1989 = 100)	65	71

Derived from Lavigne, 1999:284–287

Although industrial output had since 1989 fallen more sharply in the Czech provinces than in Slovakia, Slovaks appeared considerably poorer (in terms of GDP per head) and had suffered a far higher rate of unemployment. Economic disagreements mingled with nationalistic sentiments and a more overt continuity of the political elite in Slovakia. What emerged in Slovakia therefore was an authoritarian regime, with power closely associated with the former *nomenklatura*. The problems of transition moreover were far more intractable in Slovakia than in the Czech Republic.

Management in Slovakia

The general context of organizational and managerial transformation has been different in a number of respects from that in the Czech Republic. In spite of extensive industrialization since the Second World War, 'Many remnants of traditional agrarian society . . . are evident in Slovakia' (Letiche, 1998:221). For example, a middle class is relatively sparse and the rate of growth of small and medium enterprises has been approximately half that of the Czech Republic (Bygate, 1998:202). Slovak society is accordingly more openly structured around managers/owners and workers, between whom there is a large gap (Letiche, 1998:222).

Privatization has in consequence taken a particular direction in Slovakia, with a greater incidence of management buy-outs as the former elite has sought to retain its power through ownership and control of economic organizations. Organizations, moreover, are viewed predominantly as sources of power for the few rather than as a means to achieve goals which are broadly shared by the individuals working in them. In addition, organizations use a plethora of bureaucratic procedures in order to exert the control of the owners/managers over the workforce (Letiche, 1998:223). Such authoritarian behaviour is not restricted to members of the former system's senior management but is also evident among former middle and lower managers who since 1989 have attained senior managerial positions (Bygate, 1998:315).

Access to positions of authority and power is also heavily dependent on one's family and personal connections. The political clientelism of the communist regime has been replaced by a more primitive form of social behaviour in which power is dispensed and maintained by favouring individuals belonging to one's social grouping rather than opening such positions to society at large. Positions of authority thus tend to remain under the control of the existing discrete ruling group. According to Letiche (1998:223–224):

> . . . in Slovakia the manager's level of authority and power is almost always linked to his (almost all managers are men) social background, and the class position of his family. The current trend to 'management buyouts' seems to be rewarding high social status and, if anything, to be making the prospects of the 'outsiders' even bleaker.

It is therefore not surprising that the transformation in Slovakia has proceeded at a slower pace than in the Czech Republic. Whilst in the latter the overt political aim has been the achievement of a functioning market economy, in Slovakia the transformation appears driven more by the desire of the former system's elites to retain their control over the political and economic levers of power. In such a situation change tends to be held back, because organizations tend to be preoccupied with issues of internal control rather than with external circumstances and drivers such as customers, markets and international economic trends. However, such external factors cannot be ignored and companies have to make some kind of response to them, even if the response is limited by the company's unwillingness and/or inability to learn and adapt. For example, Letiche (1998:224) comments on the extreme division of labour in Slovakia which manifests itself in companies having rigidly defined functional areas which generally compete rather than cooperate with each other in achieving the company's goals.

Foreign-owned firms and firms founded by entrepreneurs are in general an exception in the setting described above. However, such firms represent only a small proportion of Slovak firms. The overall context of company transformation in Slovakia is described by Gasparikova (1998) as corporativist:

> Corporativism in post-communist countries can be defined as a system of interest intermediation in which the constituent units are organized into a limited number of singular, compulsory, non-competitive, hierarchically ordered and functionally differentiated categories, recognized or licensed by the state and granted a deliberate monopoly within their respective categories in exchange for observing certain controls on their selection of leaders and articulation of demands and supports. It is characterized by a corporativist system of production and distribution and a redistribution system based on family and friendship connections (pp. 183–184).

Conclusions

The evolution of management in the Czech and Slovak Republics since 1989 is characterized by both similarities and differences. Similarities include the widescale persistence of the former communist *nomenklatura* in leading company positions, in spite of attempts in the Czech Republic to curtail their influence. Another similarity is to be found in the style of management which continues to be strongly influenced by the tradition of scientific management and engineering. This largely technical approach to management is complemented by a marked degree of authoritarianism, which appears to pre-date the communist period.

In some respects balancing this authoritarianism is a concern for the needs of the locality in which the company is situated. This concern is reflected in the close relationships between companies and local communities, especially in smaller, one-company town situations. The technical core of management is thus situated in a context of personal relations where managers and workers frequently know each other and their respective families.

Although the Czech Republic is regarded as one of the leading countries in the post-communist transformation, this progress has been slower than many observers expected. Progress has been even slower in Slovakia. Clearly there has been a gap between official rhetoric and actual achievements. Moreover, governments have not always delivered what they have promised. In fact, contrary to what might have been expected from its 'shock therapy' policy, the Czech(oslovak) government undertook a series of measures to soften the blow of transformation. As a consequence of this, company transformation has been held back to a degree and there appear to be substantial differences in the ways that companies are managed, for example between former state-owned enterprises on the one hand and newly founded and foreign-owned companies on the other.

These observations are all the more pertinent to Slovakia, where developments have been conditioned by the particular national context. The context in Slovakia has been influenced more explicitly by a greater degree of state intervention, designed in part to cushion the impact of transformation and in part to secure the interests of the ruling elite. As a consequence management buyouts have been a far more widespread form of privatization in Slovakia.

In both countries, however, management appears on the whole slow to learn and adapt, especially with regard to dealing with external influences on firms' activities. This slow pace of adaptation is particularly evident in the Czech Republic because of its more advanced state of institutional change.

References

Arnason, J. (1993) *The Future that Failed, Origins and Destinies of the Soviet Model*, London and New York: Routledge.

Bata, T. (1992) *Knowledge in Action: the Bata System of Management*, Amsterdam: IOS Press.

Burianek, J. (1997) 'The Industrial Relations Still in Transition – A Commentary on Some Recent Studies on the Czech Case', *Journal for East European Management Studies*, 2, 2, pp. 161–72.

Bygate, S. (1998) 'Inherited Networks, Economic Embeddedness and Developments in Corporate Governance: Post-Communist Czech and Slovak Republics with Supporting Evidence from Eastern Germany' Ph.D. thesis, Loughborough University.

Clark, E. and Soulsby, A. (1999) *Organizational Change in Post-Communist Europe, Management and Transformation in the Czech Republic*, London and New York: Routledge.

Dangerfield, M. (1997) 'The Business Culture in the Czech Republic', in Bateman, M. (ed.) *Business Cultures in Central & Eastern Europe*, Oxford: Butterworth-Heinemann, pp. 1–34.

Ellenbogen, M. (1998) 'Führungs- und Managementstrukturen in der Tschechischen Republik aus der Sicht eines Praktikers', in Lang, R. (ed.) *Führungskräfte im osteuropäischen Transformationsprozeß*, III. Chemnitzer Ostforum, Munich and Mering: Rainer Hampp, pp. 489–98.

Gasparikova, J. (1998) 'Restructuring, Privatisation and Interest Groups', in Lang, R. (ed.) *op. cit.*, pp. 179–84.

Hoffmann, V., Jirasek, J., Kubr, M. and Pitra, Z. (1996) *Czech Manager in the Process of Transformation*, Prague: National Training Fund.

Kuras, B. (1996) *Czechs and Balances, a Nation's Survival Kit*, Prague: Baronet.

Lavigne, M. (1999) *The Economics of Transition, From Socialist Economy to Market Economy*, Basingstoke and London: Macmillan, 2nd ed.

Letiche, H. (1998) 'Transition and Human Resources in Slovakia', *Personnel Review*, 27, 3, pp. 213–26.

Maly, M. and Dedina, J. (1997) 'Veränderungen im Management tschechischer Betriebe', *Journal for East European Management Studies*, 2, 1, pp. 8–21.

Maly, M. and Novy, I. (1996) 'Barrieren bei der Gestaltung der Unternehmenskulturen in tschechischen Unternehmen', in Lang, R. (ed.) *Wandel von Unternehmenskulturen in Ostdeutschland und Osteuropa*, Munich and Mering: Rainer Hampp Verlag, pp. 153–61.

Mense-Petermann, U. (1997) 'Betriebliche Restrukturierung im Ländervergleich', *Journal for East European Management Studies*, 2, 2, pp. 173–97.

Mertlik, P. (1996) 'Czech Industry: Organizational Structure, Privatization and their Consequences for its Performance', *Emergo*, 3, 1, pp. 92–104.

Mills, A. (1995) 'The Effect of the Transition from a Communist to a Market-Based Economy on Enterprises in the Czech Republic' Ph.D. thesis, Loughborough University.

Pavlica, K. and Thorpe, R. (1998) 'Managers' Perceptions of their Identity: A Comparative Study between the Czech Republic and Britain', *British Journal of Management*, 9, pp. 133–49.

Rychetnik, L. (1996) 'The Management of Labour: A Way to an Economic Miracle? The Case of Medium-sized Czech Firms', *Emergo*, 3, 1, pp. 75–91.

Savitt, R. (1998) 'Evolving Management Practices in the Czech Republic: Restructuring and Market Orientation', *Journal for East European Management Studies*, 3, 4, pp. 339–54.

Trick, R. (1999) 'Managerial Ethics in East Central and Eastern Europe: The Case of the Czech Republic', in Edwards, V. (ed.) Proceedings of the Fifth Annual Conference on *The Impact of Transformation on Individuals, Organizations, Society*, Chalfont St Giles: CREEB, vol. 2, pp. 659–69.

Wiskemann, E. (1966) *Europe of the Dictators 1919–1945*, London: Collins.

Zauberman, A. (1976) 'Russia and Eastern Europe 1920–1970', in Cipolla, C. (ed.) *The Fontana Economic History of Europe, Contemporary Economies – 2*, Glasgow: Fontana/Collins, pp. 577–623.

Zeleny, M. (1993) 'Reforms in Czechoslovakia: Traditions or Cosmopolitanism?', in Mayurama, M. (ed.) *Management Reform in Eastern and Central Europe*, Aldershot: Dartmouth, pp. 45–64.

CHAPTER 6

Romania

Introduction

At the demise of the communist regime at the very end of 1989 Romania emerged as the poorest of the former members of COMECON. Prior to the Second World War the Romanian economy had been largely agricultural, complemented by a productive raw materials industry (for example, in petrochemicals). The communist regime which formally seized power in 1948 transformed Romania's economy with a determined and persistent focus on heavy industry which altered dramatically the economic structure of the country. This economic transformation went hand in hand with a political process of creating a socialist society which had particular Romanian characteristics. The Romanian communists at an early stage of their political power emphasized the national and nationalistic elements of their policies and resisted, wherever possible, attempts to integrate Romania into a cohesive economic or political framework under Soviet hegemony. The singularity of the Romanian approach became increasingly evident under the regime of Nicolae Ceausescu (1965–89) who from 1967 on was both head of the Communist Party and Head of State. Under Ceausescu Romania pursued economic and foreign policies which were to a large extent independent of those of the Soviet Union. For example, Romania opposed the Soviet-inspired invasion of Czechoslovakia in 1968 and sought close relationships with both the West and China. This independent stance was initially met with considerable support in the West. For example, Romania received financial support from the United Nations to found a national management development centre in 1967 (Granick, 1975:456).

In the economic sphere there was determined opposition to Soviet proposals and the prime goal of Romanian economic policy was to create a base of heavy industry. Further planks of economic policy in the 1980s were to pay off all outstanding foreign debts and to urbanize the rural areas. These economic and foreign policies were conducted in an environment of increasingly intense internal repression and the personality cult of Nicolae Ceausescu himself. This personality cult manifested itself in numerous forms, for instance, a dependence on Ceausescu personally for all significant and many minor decisions, widespread nepotism and numerous excesses such as grandiose urban planning schemes and a luxuriant, exorbitant lifestyle for those in power. Antal (1995:122), referring to the cult's impact on the workplace, speaks of 'a work culture where everything was imposed from above, the directors blind apostles of a mad God. The Old Testament had been replaced by the New Five Year Plan, and the words of Ceausescu became the nation's Bible'.

The repercussions of the Ceausescu period were manifold. The structure of the Romanian economy was fundamentally altered; moreover, the preponderance of heavy industry was in no way appropriate to the needs of the population or the post-1989 liberalized economy. The 'export drive' of the 1980s had resulted in rationing of many Romanian products (including energy). A decade of economic hardship represented a form of 'shock therapy' which made the majority of Romanians unwilling to accept further sufferings after the end of the regime. On the contrary, people were looking forward to enjoying the promised benefits of democracy and the free market.

Furthermore, the oppressive nature of the Romanian style of communism had tended to stifle any individual initiative as people had grown accustomed to waiting for instructions to be given them by their superiors. The situation in Romania at the end of 1989 has been succinctly summarized by Treptow (1997:567–69):

> Therefore, in December 1989, Romania emerged from Communist rule with a population whose standards of living had been depressed to hitherto unseen levels during a decade of falling incomes, and with a hypercentralized economy suffering from macroeconomic imbalances, severe resource misallocation, widespread shortages of both consumer products and raw materials, efficiency problems, a depreciated and largely obsolete capital base, a demoralized and weary labour force, and a collapsing infrastructure. Moreover, it lacked the managerial capacities and information about the configuration of a market economy, acquired elsewhere through previous partial attempts at economic reform and liberalization, which would have ensured a smoother path for economic transformation.

Communist transformation

At the end of the Second World War Romania was still a predominantly rural society, with almost three quarters of the population living in rural areas. In 1938, just before the onset of war, less than 10 per cent of the labour force had been employed in industry. The communist regime implemented the mainstream economic policies associated with the Soviet model such as nationalization of private property and collectivization of the agricultural sector. What developed from the 1950s and particularly under Ceausescu, however, was 'the most sustained and aberrant version of autonomous Stalinism' (Arnason, 1993:147).

By 1980 Romania had developed a substantial foundation of heavy industry and 50 per cent of national GDP now derived from industrial activities. Romania's industrial base was, however, out of all proportion to the needs of the country. Moreover, it became increasingly difficulty to sustain industry's demand for raw materials and other inputs and Romania was consequently forced to import energy and raw materials. Up to 1970 Romania had been a net exporter of energy and raw materials. In the 1980s, however, Romania needed to export more and more of its output in order to pay for imports. The expansion of exports was fuelled in part by constantly curtailing domestic consumption. The 1980s was the decade of Ceausescu's 'shock therapy' (Shen, 1997).

The relative prosperity and openness of the 1970s had thus given way to brutal internal repression and rationing for the vast majority of the population as the regime sought to stifle all forms of dissent and to repay its foreign loans.

A slow transformation since 1989

Romania's economy in the 1990s has been characterized by a slow pace of transformation. Numerous commentators have questioned the nature of the events which led to the toppling of Ceausescu and his regime, arguing that 'the former communist elite managed to retain its political and economic power' (Stan, 1997:127). A deputy minister, commenting on the extensiveness of Romania's difficulties, stated that 'During the revolution in 1989, the Romanian political, economic and administrative system – and the country's balance of values – disintegrated, creating a political and social void virtually overnight' (*Info Phare*, 1995). Other commentators take a more positive view of developments, seeing in the slow advance of transformation government policies aimed at protecting the population, which had just emerged from a decade of deprivations, from further hardship and offering them a certain level of social protection and social peace (Shen, 1997:83).

The lack of a clear break in terms of the political elite has been compounded by the general appearance of indecisiveness on the part of politicians when it comes to issues of economic restructuring. Certainly, the Romanian economy under communism was highly centralized and this has made the task of privatizing state-owned enterprises, particularly the large *regies autonomes* which were to all intents and purposes monopolies, extremely difficult. At the same time, where privatization has been carried through, there is evidence of abuses of positions of privilege, granting of political favours and of managers exploiting their knowledge as insiders to acquire shares in enterprises with a high probability of success in the new environment (Shen, 1997:133). Not surprisingly management and employee buyout (MEBO) has emerged as the most common form of privatization.

A decade after the collapse of the communist regime Romania was still one of the poorest countries in Europe, along with Albania, Bulgaria and parts of the former Yugoslavia, when relative prosperity is measured by GDP per head of population. A further indicator of Romania's economic situation, at least from the viewpoint of foreign investors, is the volume of FDI which has entered the country. In this respect too Romania has fared in a similar manner to the previously mentioned countries, attracting in the period 1989–97 one of the lowest levels of per capita FDI in the region (EBRD, 1998:17).

Other economic indicators tend to confirm the image of a country struggling with enormous difficulties which include high inflation and a shrinking economy. Although the private sector accounted for 58 per cent of GDP in 1997, there has been substantial deindustrialization, with industrial output below 60 per cent of its 1990 level by 1998 (*Wirtschaftslage und Reformprozesse in Mittel- und Osteuropa*, 1999:72). Rising unemployment was partially masked by involvement in the shadow economy and subsistence agriculture.

National culture

Romanian national identity has evolved over a considerable period of time and has drawn on a variety of influences. The territory of modern Romania corresponds to part of the former Roman province of Dacia, and the modern Romanian language is largely derived from Latin. In Romanian culture, modern-day Romanians are seen as the descendants of the Romanized inhabitants of Dacia and as members of the wider Latin world.

This cultural adherence to the notion of a Latin world has differentiated Romanians from their Slav and Hungarian neighbours. This aspect also differentiated the Romanians from the Ottomans who ruled the country for more than 300 years after the Battle of Mohács in 1526 even though Ottoman rule was conducted in the eighteenth century indirectly through Phanariots (Greeks loyal to the Ottoman Empire) as well as by members of the local Romanian nobility.

The achievement of an independent Romanian state, however, did not come about until 1878, with the union and recognition as a sovereign state of the

Romanian provinces of Moldavia and Wallachia. By the early 1920s Romania had expanded substantially. It had been on the side of the victorious Allies in the First World War (1914–18) and consequently gained considerable other territories including Transylvania (from Hungary) and Bessarabia (from Russia). As a consequence of this expansion Romania had become a multi-ethnic state. In the period between the two world wars (1918–1939) nearly one quarter of the population of Romania consisted of other nationalities (Wiskemann, 1966:267).

In the Second World War (1939–45) Romania fought on the side of Nazi Germany until 1944 when it switched its allegiance. At the end of the war it was obliged to cede considerable territory (including Bessarabia) to the Soviet Union. As a consequence the proportion of ethnic minorities declined substantially and now accounts for around 10 per cent of the overall population. The largest minority ethnic group in Romania since the end of the First World War has been the Hungarian community, concentrated predominantly in central and south-eastern Transylvania. It is therefore important to bear in mind when discussing Romanian national culture that the Romanian state comprises a substantial minority which is ethnically not Romanian and adheres to alternative cultural values.

A second defining characteristic of Romanian culture is the religious adherence to the Greek Orthodox form of Christianity. According to Catana and Catana (1999:257) who in their analysis of Romanian culture applied the cultural audit system of the twentieth-century Romanian philosopher and poet Lucian Blaga, the Greek Orthodox religion has been influential in developing characteristics of gentleness and passivity among Romanians.

Catana and Catana (1999) identify further characteristics of Romanian culture including a clear separation of home and work, a time horizon focused predominantly on the present and an aversion to taking decisions. The separation of home and work can be understood as a feature of a society which displays a high regard for communal values. The family takes precedence over external relationships with, for example, individuals and organizations not formally linked to the family. The positive aspects of such communal values (e.g. support for family members) also have negative manifestations in practices such as unconditional support for family members (irrespective of rights and wrongs), disregard for external, civic institutions (e.g. the law and fiscal systems), nepotism and corruption.

Romanians' temporal horizon, moreover, is focused largely on the here and now, with only a limited preoccupation with future events. Such a temporal horizon clearly makes it more difficult to persuade individuals to take a longer term view of situations. The reluctance of Romanians to undergo further hardships after 1989 may have been influenced both by their experience of the 'immiserizing growth' (Daianu, 1997:95) of the 1980s and by a culturally influenced disregard for future developments. According to Lukács *et al.* (1999)

traditionalism, reflecting centuries of peasant life, and nationalism are the dominant feature of Romanian culture. Although traditionalism has been affected by industrialization and urbanization the authors refer to 'Romanian citizens whom history has taught to be strongly nationalist, with a mentality of resistance to change, mistrustful towards work and performance values' (Lukács *et al.*, 1999:14). The reluctance to come to a decision, moreover, results in lengthy and inconclusive meetings (Catana and Catana, 1999:255).

Business culture

Clearly these dimensions of the national culture have also influenced business culture in Romania. Campbell (2000) refers to the notion of an 'Official Romanian Culture' which evolved among the professional middle classes after independence in the latter part of the nineteenth century and was particularly prevalent in government organizations and large companies. This 'Official Romanian Culture' was particularly inspired by a strong cultural relationship with France. Campbell (2000:321–322) describes the main features of this culture in the following way:

> In managerial terms what has been termed here as Official Romanian Culture may be taken to mean the following: a high level of courtesy (kissing a woman's hand on introduction is still considered standard practice) but a generally formal tone in conversation; elegant speechmaking (still much appreciated in meetings and conferences) combined with vagueness about what has been agreed at meetings; the ability to engage in polite bureaucratic obfuscation; a tendency towards backroom deals and intrigues, usually carried out with brisk efficiency and eloquently rationalized; a high degree of networking; careful observance of hierarchical niceties combined with unforced bonhomie; a strong emphasis on symbols, protocol and elegant written communication combined with a lack of structure in the management process, strong differences of status between superiors and subordinates; a strong professional ethos particularly in law, engineering and architecture; a certain preference for words over deeds; a strong capacity for abstract thought, but less for practical entrepreneurialism.

This 'Official Romanian Culture' persisted under communism as many officials stayed in post after the change of political system in the late 1940s. The communist regime moreover emphasized Romania's national version of socialist development. Taylor (1999:57) also notes that business in Romania continues to be conducted in ways 'which are comparable to Italian and French models'.

Managers

The professional background of Romanian managers is predominantly in engineering. According to Olaru (1998) 68 per cent of managers have qualifications in engineering; 21 per cent have a qualification in economics. In general, knowledge of accounting and finance is regarded as weak. In 1995 a Romanian state secretary commented that:

> Here in Romania, the vast majority of management personnel are engineering minded. They know little about [market-based] economic phenomena. And they do not understand the reasons behind fiscal or monetary policy adjustments. (Shen, 1997:48)

Managers, moreover, are perceived less as professionals than as leaders. In this respect managers perform a social as well as an economic function (Gehmann, 1996:220). Since managers are perceived primarily as leaders, professionalism and level and type of education are secondary to criteria such as experience and ability to meet other people's expectations. These expectations include maintaining job security and providing employment for family and friends. Externally, managing directors are expected to maintain good relationships with their counterparts in other companies (for example, on the issue of inter-enterprise debt) and with those in governmental organizations (Gehmann, 1996).

This social dimension of the manager's role often conflicts with the achievement of economic objectives as embodied in Western business values (Kelemen and Gardiner, 1999:280). For example, Romanian managers may feel obliged to employ members of their family and be reluctant to dismiss employees who would be considered redundant from a purely economic rationale. This tension between social and economic objectives consequently has an impact on the nature and speed of change within Romanian organizations (about which more will be said later).

Within organizations management style tends to be autocratic. Manifestations of individual initiative are limited and superiors expect obedience from their subordinates. Individual initiative appears circumscribed to a greater extent in private companies than in state-owned enterprises as private owners (often also doubling as the managing director) exert their personal power and authority (Catana and Catana, 1996). Kelemen (1999:203) illustrates the persistence of the top-down approach to decision-making and management with a quotation from the general director of a textile company:

> I want to know all that's happening. I don't trust my subordinates. I need to be in control all the time, otherwise things will go wrong.

Management practices thus appear stuck in many respects in traditional patterns of behaviour. Understandably this is the preferred course of action of managers who had built up their experience under the former regime. According to Stan (1997:136):

> The managers who were skillful enough to retain their positions in the aftermath of the 1989 uprising sought to either seek assistance from the ministries to which they were formerly subordinated (for applying pressure on former suppliers to maintain their sales, obtaining critical inputs, setting advantageous prices, granting subsidies, and facilitating the extension of credit to finance production) or look for other ways to survive on the market (such as laying off some workers and placing others on extended vacations, or resurrecting old networks in an attempt to continue the pre-1989 patterns of purchases and sales in the absence of necessary funds).

The barriers to corporate and managerial transformation are also discussed by Catana *et al.* (1999). In a study of 200 senior managers conducted in Transylvania in 1997, the authors identify a considerable resistance to change and a strong inclination to preserve the status quo. The extent of resistance to change was positively correlated with the company's size and its importance to the national economy. This resistance to change appears influenced by a number of factors, including a possible feeling of managerial incompetence, the legacy of practices from the former regime, a general fear of change, the stress of decision-making under the evolving and more market-orientated conditions and perceived threats to managers' personal image. In the survey lower-level managers were identified as being particularly reluctant to change and acted as an impediment to organizational transformation. Catana *et al.* (1999:151–152) explain the resistance to change from the perspective of the national culture, commenting:

> Romanians, as a group, seek stability, fear uncertainty and avoid risk. Romanian managers tend to procrastinate and react to situations rather than taking a proactive approach to their environment. Long-run planning is limited to a risk-free process of creating 'daydream scenarios' which are unlikely to materialize.

Company transformation, although taking a variety of forms in terms of strategy (Kelemen and Hristov, 1998), appears in a majority of cases motivated predominantly by the necessity to survive rather than by strategies based on product-market considerations. According to Kelemen (1999:202) no more than 10 per cent of Romanian organizations have embarked on any significant economic restructuring.

Intimations of change

In spite of an overall picture of resistance to change, there is evidence that the circumstances of Romanian managers and their organizations are not static. Pressures for change emanate from external influences on the Romanian economy and to a certain degree from foreign companies operating within Romania.

While features of the old systems such as cronyism, nepotism and politically inspired appointments persist (Kelemen, 1999:206), there are also indications of a small number of companies enacting cultural change (Kelemen and Hristov, 1998). Olaru (1998) has, for example, identified some change in the style of management since 1990. The managers elected in 1990 largely with trade union support, tended to persist with the autocratic practices inherited from the former regime. Their primary aim was to maintain levels of employment and avoid antagonizing the trades unions. They generally stayed in post for only one or two years. These managers then tended to be replaced by managers who adopted a more conciliatory management style and developed survival strategies for their organizations. Although compared with their predecessors, their approach was considered conciliatory, they could also be tough and inflexible when such an approach was deemed necessary.

Dumitrescu (1997) has also noted some development of managerial practices in his study of Romanian managers employed in the Bucharest subsidiaries of foreign multi-national corporations. Dumitrescu solicited the views of both Romanian and foreign managers. The Romanian managers valued characteristics such as authority without authoritarianism, i.e. knowing when to be the boss but also acting as a 'good father figure'; communication (regarded as a weakness because of the communist legacy of giving and taking orders); and multidisciplinary business knowledge (the majority of the interviewees had come from an engineering background but now held positions in finance, sales and marketing). A weakness identified by the respondents was the existence of a defensive, wait-and-see attitude. This attitude appeared to derive from a tendency to regard external forces as dominant.

The foreign managers characterized their Romanian colleagues as autocratic paternalists, status seekers, weak on administration and with a tendency to regard knowledge more highly than skills. This last-mentioned characteristic was considered to be changing. Another feature identified in the survey was the perception of a decline in managers' authority, occasioned by an increasing use of delegation in companies which had experienced growth. While many features of traditional Romanian business culture (for example, communal relationships and nepotism) were still evident, the Romanian managers in the survey had clearly had to make concessions to the expectations of their foreign employers (for example, in the form of a higher degree of individual assertiveness and a growing recognition of the value of skills as well as knowledge).

Conclusions

On the whole, evaluations of corporate and managerial change in Romania since the fall of communism have tended to be pessimistic. According to Kelemen (1999:207):

... managers have not changed their way of managing in a significant way. They run allegedly successful organizations, but they have achieved such success through old ways of management. Such old ways consist of personal contacts, intuition, interpersonal skills and other muddling-through strategies of managing.

Numerous factors have combined to hinder the process of change. First, the broad cultural context has facilitated policies of limited action. The persistence of communal values holds back the implementation of policies which might be considered necessary and rational from an economic point of view but might also have far-reaching and negative social consequences (e.g. high levels of redundancies). A time horizon focused predominantly on the present is also unlikely to encourage consideration of longer-term, strategic issues. These factors go hand in hand with a reliance on personal relationships which can be called upon in certain circumstances to stave off the consequences of economic activity (for instance, personal relationships may be called upon to invalidate the rational economic consequences of expanding inter-enterprise debt). The cultural context moreover is not conducive to decision making and risk taking, so that all in all the cultural context acts as one barrier to individual and organizational change.

Second, the political context has tended to concede the need for change rather than promote it. The survival of large sections of the former communist elite has tended to be one factor exerting pressure against change. The new political elite has failed to emerge in sufficient strength and with sufficient authority to counteract the influence of the old elite. In fact, the political climate has often been typified by internal squabbles between parties who manifestly are supposed to be and should be working in concert for the overall benefit of the country. The political context has also been conditioned by a fear of social unrest, occasioned by a too rapid transformation of the economy.

Third, the inherited industrial structure has been a genuine impediment. Because of its concentration on traditional heavy industries and high degree of centralization, the Romanian economy had possibly far more handicaps at the start of transition than many of its COMECON counterparts. At the same time the high degree of centralization excluded any initiatives involving enterprise autonomy and managerial discretion as had occurred, even if only to a limited degree, in some of the other COMECON countries.

Fourth, managerial self-image also acts as a barrier to change. Managers value knowledge and experience above skills, and consequently there is a tendency to continue to rely on traditional patterns of action and behaviour. An engineering bias still persists, with managers concentrating on raising productivity. Marketing and sales are moreover regarded by managers as low-status activities (Lascu *et al.*, 1997:188). On the whole managers perceive themselves as leaders rather than professionals, a viewpoint which downplays the importance of a repertoire of knowledge and skills which are appropriate to the new circumstances.

Although the barriers to change have proved particularly potent, there are some indications of pressures for change emanating from international and domestic sources. Even though Romania has attracted relatively little foreign direct investment, a number of multinational consumer goods companies have established a presence in Romania – it is after all the second largest market in CEE in terms of population (over 22 million). Another foreign investor has been Daewoo in the automobile industry. Foreign investors have brought in new knowledge and technologies and, even though largely concentrated in Bucharest, are beginning to influence the way Romanian companies and managers operate.

Second, the privatization process in spite of its slow pace is helping to create a new class of owners and entrepreneurs whose interests are aligned with achieving economic success. Owners and entrepreneurs are more likely to be driven primarily by the need to survive and prosper rather than by other extra-economic considerations.

A third driver of change is the overall poor performance of the economy, the deteriorating general standard of living and increasing disparities with the more successful transforming economies of the region. As the present becomes more and more unsatisfactory for a rising proportion of Romanians, there may be an increasing pressure for radical change in order to improve the future situation.

Fourth, at the corporate level there is evidence that companies are having to change in order to adapt to the new circumstances and survive. Vatamanu (1998) and Gavril and Vatamanu (1999) have described the process of transformation at the Galati steel complex which was one of the showpieces of Romania's drive to establish heavy industry. The Galati steel complex is by far the largest steel producer in Romania employing over 36 000 workers in 1995 and 1996. Transformation at the steel complex has been driven by external forces such as the tariff relationship with the EU (and aspirations to EU membership), reducing tariffs on steel imports into Romania and the general evolution of demand for Romanian steel. In 1996 Romanian steel consumption was only just over one quarter of its 1989 level. Drastically reducing domestic demand in conjunction with a general global stagnation in demand for steel has resulted in a manifest need to improve the financial structure and technological basis of steel production at Galati. This transformation has involved updating the technology used at the plant and establishing a number of joint ventures with foreign companies in the areas of production and sales. Whilst the authors focus on the technological and to a certain extent financial aspects of the transformation, no indication is given of any transformation in terms of organization structure, management and human resources.

Finally, there appears to be recognition at governmental level that Romanian management needs to change (Kelemen, 1999). Olaru (1998) also postulates the need for a new kind of manager who is inventive and a participative reformer. In the light of developments since 1989 it is most likely that managerial transformation in Romania will evolve in a slow and fragmentary manner.

References

Antal, D. (1995) *Out of Romania*, London: Faber and Faber.

Arnason, J. (1993) *The Future that Failed, Origins and Destinies of the Soviet Model*, London and New York: Routledge.

Campbell, A. (2000) 'Management in Romania', in Warner, M. (ed.), IEBM *Regional Encyclopaedia of Business & Management: Management in Europe*, London: Business Press, pp. 319–28.

Catana, A. and Catana, D. (1999) 'Romanian Cultural Background and its Relevance for Cross-Cultural Management', *Journal for East European Management Studies*, 4, 3, pp. 252–58.

Catana, D. and Catana, A. (1996) 'Aspects of Transformation of Corporate Cultures in Romania', in Lang, R. (ed.), *Wandel von Unternehmenskulturen in Ostdeutschland und Osteuropa*, Munich and Mering: Rainer Hampp Verlag, pp. 195–208.

Catana, D., Catana, A. and Finlay, J. (1999) 'Managerial Resistance to Change: Romania's Quest for a Market Economy', *Journal for East European Management Studies*, 4, 2, pp. 149–64.

Daianu, D. (1997) 'Macro-Economic Stabilization in Post-Communist Romania', in Stan, L. (ed.), *Romania in Transition*, Aldershot: Dartmouth, pp. 93–125.

Dumitrescu, M.-F. (1997) 'Attitudes of Romanian Managers towards Business, as Reflected by the Romanian National Culture. A Foreign Enterprise Perspective', Unpublished MA dissertation, Chalfont St Giles: Buckinghamshire College of Higher Education/Brunel University.

EBRD (1998) *Annual Report 1997*, London: EBRD.

Gavril, E. and Vatamanu, L. (1999) 'The International Transfer of Technology and Joint Ventures in the Process of Restructuring the Romanian Metallurgical Industries', in Edwards, V. (ed.), Proceedings of the Fifth Annual Conference on *The Impact of Transformation on Individuals, Organizations, Society*, Chalfont St Giles: CREEB, pp. 257–66.

Gehmann, U. (1996) 'Corporate Culture in Transition – Aspects of Organizational Behaviour and Related Socioeconomic Consequences', in Lang, R. (ed.), *Wandel von Unternehmenskulturen in Ostdeutschland und Osteuropa*, Munich and Mering: Rainer Hampp Verlag, pp. 209–26.

Granick, D. (1975) *Enterprise Guidance in Eastern Europe, A Comparison of Four Socialist Economies*, Princeton: Princeton University Press.

Info Phare (1995) February.

Kelemen, M. (1999) 'The Myth of Restructuring: "Competent" Managers and the Transition to a Market Economy: a Romanian Tale', *British Journal of Management*, 10, pp. 199–208.

Kelemen, M. and Gardiner, K. (1999) 'Paradoxes of Managerial Work: the Case of Ghana and Romania', in Edwards, V. (ed.), Proceedings of the Fifth Annual Conference on *The Impact of Transformation on Individuals, Organizations, Society*, Chalfont St Giles: CREEB, pp. 278–97.

Kelemen, M. and Hristov, L. (1998) 'From Centrally Planned Culture to Entrepreneurial Culture: The Example of Bulgarian and Romanian Organisations', *Journal for East European Management Studies*, 3, 3, pp. 216–26.

Lukács, E., Nicolai, M. and Hincu, R-Z. (1999) 'The Impact of Advertising on the Population of Romania', *Journal of European Business Education*, 8, 2, pp. 11–26.

Lascu, D-N., Ahmed, Z. and Vatasecu, M. (1997) 'Applications of the Marketing Concept Philosophy in Romania', in Stan, L. (ed.), *Romania in Transition*, Aldershot: Dartmouth, pp. 183–90.

Olaru, A. (1998) 'The Attitude Towards Change of Romanian Managers in the Transition to Market Economy', in Lang, R. (ed.), *Führungskräfte im osteuropäischen Transformationsprozeß*, III. Chemnitzer Ostforum, Munich and Mering, pp. 313–20.

Shen, R. (1997) *The Restructuring of Romania's Economy, A Paradigm of Flexibility and Adaptability*, Westport, Connecticut and London: Praeger.

Stan, L. (1997) 'Romanian Privatization Program: Catching Up with the East', in Stan, L. (ed.), *Romania in Transition*, Aldershot: Dartmouth, pp. 127–61.

Taylor, A. (1999) 'Business Culture', in Jolly, A. and Kettaneh, N. (eds.), *Doing Business in Romania*, London: CBI/Kogan Page, pp. 53–57.

Treptow, W. (ed.), (1997) *A History of Romania*, Iasi: The Center for Romanian Studies.

Vatamanu, O. (1998) 'The Management of Transition in the Metallurgical Industry in the Light of Romania's Integration in the European Union', in Edwards, V. (ed.), Proceedings of the Fourth Annual Conference on *Convergence or Divergence: Aspirations and Reality in Central and Eastern Europe and Russia*, Chalfont St Giles: CREEB, pp. 224–30.

Wirtschaftslage und Reformprozesse in Mittel- und Osteuropa (1999) Berlin: Bundesministerium für Wirtschaft und Technologie.

Wiskemann, E. (1966) *Europe of the Dictators 1919–1945*, London: Collins.

CHAPTER 7

Bulgaria

Throughout the period of communist rule (1944–90) Bulgaria was the most loyal and placid ally of the Soviet Union and has been described as a 'byword for acquiescence and conformity with the Soviet model' (Crampton, 1997:241). In Bulgaria there was no rejection of the Soviet model as in Yugoslavia and Albania, no threatening attempts to create socialism with a human face as in the Prague Spring, no national deviation as in Romania, no popular uprisings as in East Germany in 1953, Hungary in 1956 or widespread popular opposition movements such as Solidarity in Poland. While the Plovdiv tobacco workers did go on strike in 1953 (Crampton, 1997:195) and the collectivization of agriculture was imposed on Bulgarian farmers, Bulgaria stands out for the relative lack of concern it caused the Soviet Union. In fact, Bulgaria did very little to give the Soviet Union any disquiet and on occasions it appeared more subservient than even the Soviet Union found comfortable, for example, when it expressed the wish of actually becoming a member of the USSR.

Bulgaria and Russia

There are a number of explanations for Bulgaria's close attachment to the Soviet Union and, more specifically to Russia. Bulgarian Russophilia has a long tradition and is based more than on purely ethnic and religious affinities, although the fact that both Bulgarians and Russians are Orthodox Slavs and use the Cyrillic alphabet has been without doubt a contributory factor. One major reason for Bulgarians' attachment to Russia derives from the role played by Russia in the nineteenth century in freeing Bulgaria from Ottoman rule.

Bulgaria had been a major independent kingdom in the ninth and tenth centuries (852–1018) and in the thirteenth and fourteenth centuries (1185–1396). In the period between the First and Second Kingdoms Bulgaria had been a part of the Byzantine Empire. In 1396, however, the Second Kingdom fell to the

Ottoman invaders and became a part of the Ottoman Empire for nearly 500 years. The experience of Ottoman rule had a dramatic effect on Bulgarian culture and society because of its severity and long duration. The Bulgarian revival of the nineteenth century sought to halt the decay of the national culture and re-establish an independent Bulgaria. It was directed not only against Ottoman rule but also against the influence of Greek culture disseminated by the Orthodox Church. The revival was strongly supported by Russia (which was competing with the Ottoman Empire for control of the Black Sea area and from there access to the Mediterranean). Conflicts of interest resulted in the Russo-Turkish War as a result of which, by the Treaty of Berlin in 1878, Bulgaria was re-created as a principality subject to the Sultan. Southern Bulgaria (Eastern Rumelia) remained an Ottoman province. With the decline of Ottoman power Bulgaria and Eastern Rumelia were able to unite under the same ruler in 1885 and full independence was finally declared in 1908. Many Bulgarians were consequently grateful and indebted to Russia for the significant role it played in liberating Bulgaria from centuries of Ottoman rule.

The Russians were also regarded as liberating Bulgaria towards the end of the Second World War. Bulgaria had played an ambiguous role in the Second World War. Although joining the Axis Powers in 1940, Bulgaria sought to limit its involvement as much as possible, for example, resisting participating in German military action against the Soviet Union and refusing to send Bulgarian Jews to death camps. The arrival of Soviet troops in Bulgaria in September 1944 was warmly received by the local population and they were given 'a wildly enthusiastic welcome' (Crampton, 1997:183).

Origins of acquiescence

Although Bulgarian Russophilia is a significant phenomenon, other factors contributed to Bulgaria's acquiescence under communism. Bulgaria before the Second World War had been a largely agricultural country, with only pockets of significant urban and industrial development. Nevertheless, the Bulgarian Communist Party had attracted some support (and a ban) in the inter-war period. In the elections following World War One it had polled around one fifth of the popular vote. Following an abortive attempt at insurrection the Bulgarian Communist Party was banned in 1923. Popular support for the Party was, however, not diminished by this action and it took control of Sofia city council in 1932 (Crampton, 1997:149–61). The communist takeover of Bulgaria which effectively began in 1944, when the Red Army entered Bulgarian territory, built on the communists' domestic support and the widespread historical and contemporary support for Russia.

Another factor contributing to the acquiescence of Bulgaria within the Soviet bloc was the genuine rise in living standards experienced by the population, at least until the 1970s. Economically, Bulgarians had to bear numerous hardships under Ottoman rule and the Bulgarian economy had endured various difficulties since independence. Whatever their objections to the political policies of the communist regime, it was difficult to deny that in the first 25 years of its existence the regime had increased the economic standard of living of the vast majority of the population. According to official statistics, albeit very questionable ones, Bulgaria in the late 1980s was reported as having the third-highest GDP per head in CEE, with only the former GDR and Czechoslovakia recording higher figures (Lavigne, 1999:48).

A further factor inhibiting opposition to the communist regime was the long-established Bulgarian tradition of hermitism and inner immigration (Crampton, 1997:238–41). There was a strong tradition of hermitism in medieval Bulgaria. Moreover, some of the characteristics associated with such movements were given encouragement by Ottoman rule. Individuals, if at all possible, sought to disassociate themselves from the harsh realities of the world in which they lived, seeking solace and consolation in contemplation and withdrawal. This cultural characteristic appears to have contributed to the acquiescence of Bulgarians under communism as opposition to the regime was vented not in open manifestations of dissent but rather by a withdrawal into the comfort and security of one's own self. Although this phenomenon was also evident in other communist countries, in Bulgaria it had deep-rooted cultural foundations.

The Soviet model

The introduction and implementation of the Soviet model in Bulgaria followed the general pattern of events in the region. Communist regimes (initially broad-based patriotic coalitions) assumed control with the support of the Red Army. In due course the coalition parties were emasculated or destroyed. By the end of 1947 Bulgaria was to all intents and purposes a one-party state. The economic policies of the Bulgarian communists had three major strands: nationalization of economic assets, collectivization of agriculture and heavy industrialization. In 1949 the first Five Year Plan was introduced.

Bulgaria in the mid to late 1940s had been a still largely agricultural society, with around 80 per cent of the population working on the land. Unlike the general situation of most of CEE, however, land ownership had tended to demonstrate a high degree of egalitarianism. Most of the rural population tended to be small landowners; there were therefore only few large landowners. Consequently the Communist Party had little scope to gain popularity by redistributing land from large landowners to formerly landless labourers as had happened, for example, in East Germany. The Agrarian Party furthermore had traditionally played a significant role in Bulgarian politics, indicating the strength of the small landowners as a political constituency. However, the Agrarians were destroyed as an independent party by the Communists, remaining formally the communists' coalition partner throughout the period of communist rule (i.e. up to 1990). Though the move to collectivize agriculture was fiercely resisted by the peasant farmers up to the early 1950s, the collectivization process was declared completed in 1958 (Crampton, 1997:196).

While collectivization fundamentally changed the essence of Bulgarian agriculture, the policy of heavy industrialization transformed Bulgaria's industrial and social structure. As a result of this policy Bulgaria evolved from an agricultural, rural society into an industrial and urban one. In 1948 only 8 per cent of the workforce had been employed in industry. By 1960 this had risen to 22 per cent and by 1987 to 38 per cent. Over the period 1948–87 employment in agriculture had fallen from 82 to 19 per cent of total employment. This change in the structure of economic activity was also reflected in the changing relative contributions to net material product (NMP), the socialist economies' equivalent of GDP. Agriculture's share of NMP declined from 59 to 12 per cent over the period 1948–89, while that of industry more than doubled from 23 to 57 per cent (Bristow, 1996:10 and 20). Under the industrialization policy moreover, Bulgaria developed major branches of industry such as steel, machine building, metalworking, textile production and food processing – all this in a country which before the Second World War had had no engineering plants. One of the consequences of industrialization was that by the mid 1970s around three fifths of the population lived in the urban areas. By 1990 two thirds of the population lived in towns and cities (Petrova *et al.*, 1991).

The concept of industrialization was also applied to agricultural production, especially from the late 1960s (Bristow, 1996:11). Units of production became increasingly larger through amalgamation of collectives, with each so-called agro-industrial complex employing a minimum of 6000 people.

The transformation of the domestic economy went hand in hand with integration within COMECON. Bulgaria's international economic relations were in fact characterized by a high degree of integration in COMECON. Bulgaria was possibly the most highly integrated of the COMECON members. Within COMECON Bulgaria was a major supplier of food products, although it also specialized in items such as fork-lift trucks and later in some computing products. Overall Bulgaria appears to have gained from its role within COMECON and benefited from COMECON schemes for specialization.

Economic policy throughout the communist period was on the whole stable and does not demonstrate any of the major shifts or experiments experienced by other COMECON members such as Czechoslovakia, Hungary and Poland. Outside of the main thrust of economic policy proposed reforms were cautious and even half-hearted. For example, there had been plans to increase decentralization of industry in the mid 1960s. However, these were dropped a few years later because of the events resulting from the Prague Spring. Further reforms in the 1980s, for example, relating to workers' self-management and the election of enterprise directors were haphazard, a case of too little change being followed by an attempt at too much change. To quote Crampton (1997:213) 'In economic terms the welter of reforms in the 1980s brought little but massively destructive dislocation in economic administration . . .'

Bulgarian managers under communism

According to Todeva (2000) management developed in Bulgaria only after 1945, as the country industrialized under the communist regime. The role played by managers in the period up to 1990 thus conformed to a large degree to the Soviet model of management in that they generally acted as administrators rather than decision makers (Bristow, 1996:16). The extent of centralization over such a long period impeded the introduction of reforms as managers lacked the attitudes and capabilities to respond to situations requiring greater individual initiative as in the proposed reforms of the 1980s. This dilemma is well expressed by Crampton (1997:208):

> The most important obstacle in the path of economic advance, however, was that Bulgaria's managerial cadres were not trained for operating in a system which called for self-reliance, responsibility and the making of decisions on purely economic grounds. Managers were reluctant to buy western machines if similar Soviet ones were available because they feared they might be suspected of political disloyalty; plant managers who had for decades been used to having their production routines settled for them by central organisations often did not know how to find their own raw materials or their own markets; and producers accustomed to sacrifice everything to achieving plan totals were deaf to calls to improve the quality of their goods, particularly if that meant reducing the quantity of production.

The Bulgarian economy since 1990

The communist regime in Bulgaria dissolved rather than collapsed. Although there was increasing public opposition to the regime from environmental protesters and alternative political movements, this protest stayed within limits. Zhivkov, the *de facto* ruler of Bulgaria since 1954, when he had become party secretary, was removed by a 'palace coup' in late 1989. Bulgaria appeared to be succumbing to the sequence of events in the Soviet Union and other CEE countries rather than taking a lead to determine its own destiny. The stability of communist rule gave way to the uncertainty and volatility of democratic government as the Communist Party reformed itself and a multi-party system came into effect. In 1990, however, the Bulgarian economy bore the hallmarks of the communist party's economic policies since 1944. According to Bristow (1996:84): 'Bulgaria entered transition as the second most industrialized country in the communist world, its proportion of GDP generated by industry (almost 60 per cent) being only slightly lower than that of the former Czechoslovakia'.

A second distinguishing feature of the Bulgarian economy at the end of communism was its high dependence on trade with COMECON and in particular with the Former Soviet Union. It has been estimated that around 60 per cent of exports and 50 per cent of imports were with COMECON partners (Bristow, 1996:105). These levels of trade became no longer rational or sustainable after 1990 as the former COMECON markets declined and re-oriented their trade to Western Europe. One consequence of the demise of COMECON was a rapid decline in traditional Bulgarian exports. For example, exports of machinery and equipment had accounted for about half of Bulgarian exports in 1989. The proportion had collapsed to only 15 per cent by 1993 (Bristow, 1996:113).

Furthermore, with the end of the communist system of economic management, Bulgaria found itself saddled with a gigantic international debt, according to Crampton (1997:217) amounting to $12 billion! Such a high level of foreign currency debt and the related interest charges put enormous pressures on the Bulgarian economy and on the government's ability to obtain foreign loans in order to modernize the economy and aspects of the national infrastructure.

Not surprisingly the first ten years of democratic government were accentuated by economic crises and periods of hyper-inflation as the economic system tried to come to terms with the new realities. However, the process of economic transformation was heavily influenced by the general climate of political uncertainty and instability as successive governments, including former communists, failed to develop and implement robust political and economic policies. As Crampton (1997:220–221) has noted, by the end of 1990 'most of the apparatus of totalitarianism was dismantled. . . . But . . . democracy had not yet been constructed'. Developments since 1990 have continued to be slow.

This climate of uncertainty and instability had a clear impact on the functioning of the economy and of the enterprises within it. For instance, the process of restructuring and in particular of privatization proceeded only fitfully and at the end of 1999 official sources were still talking of accelerating the privatization process. While enterprises were decentralized and 'unbundled', thus creating a larger number of enterprises and hence a more competitive business environment, the process of privatization evolved at a slow pace. Although the private sector share of GDP was estimated at 50 per cent in mid 1997 (EBRD,

1998:12) the proportion of private sector activity is as much the outcome of a decline in overall economic activity as of the performance of privatized former state-owned enterprises and new businesses.

A further result of the general political and economic conditions has been the relatively low inflow of foreign direct investment. Cumulative FDI-inflows have amounted to $103 per capita over the period 1989–97, a figure which puts Bulgaria on the same level as Albania and Romania (EBRD, 1998:17). The relative smallness of the Bulgarian market as well as the kind of industrial assets available for privatization had tended to make potential investors consider seriously any acquisition. In addition, potential investors have had reservations about the pace of privatization and overall transformation. For example, it was not until 1993 that the first state-owned enterprise was actually sold off.

As the Bulgarian general manager of a Bulgarian-foreign joint venture commented: 'The atmosphere is difficult; you must be very brave and tough to invest in Bulgaria' (Koparanova, 1998:38). In the early 1990s the level of individual cases of FDI tended to be extremely low, with 65 per cent of investments below $2000. Interestingly, a significant proportion of investment was coming from Bulgaria's neighbours Greece and Turkey (Bobeva and Bozhkov, 1996).

The transformation of the Bulgarian economy has been further hampered by a number of external influences and events, in particular the Gulf War against Iraq in 1991, United Nations sanctions against Yugoslavia (i.e. Serbia) during the 1990s, NATO action in Kosovo in 1999 and the European Union's policy on the importation of certain products. UN sanctions against Iraq because of its invasion of Kuwait had a serious impact on Bulgaria's economic circumstances because Iraq was a major trading partner. Payment for services provided by Bulgaria was often in the form of oil shipments which became subject to the UN embargo.

Moreover, sanctions against Yugoslavia, Bulgaria's western neighbour affected adversely not only trading relations between the two countries but also interrupted the flow of traffic between north-west and south-east Europe. This route through Yugoslavia and Bulgaria had been a major trade route and of economic significance to the Bulgarian economy. The imposition of UN sanctions and the need to find alternative routes was a major problem for Bulgaria as companies avoiding Yugoslavia also tended consequently to avoid Bulgarian territory because of an absence of a viable alternative route via Bulgaria.

Thirdly, Bulgaria faced considerable problems in re-orienting its trade towards Western Europe. Bulgaria had been particularly dependent on trade with its COMECON partners and had therefore made fewer inroads into EU markets than some of the other COMECON members. Attempts to achieve greater penetration in the EU markets were also frustrated by the EU restrictions on certain so-called 'sensitive' goods which included products in which Bulgaria had a certain comparative advantage as, for example, foodstuffs and textiles.

Corporate restructuring

As mentioned earlier, corporate restructuring has been held back by the slow pace of privatization and the low level of interest shown by foreign investors. There was considerable debate about the whole issue of privatization, for example, with regard to safeguarding the interests of employees. Early attempts at privatization encountered difficulties, in part because the relevant legislation had not always been appropriately drafted (Bristow, 1996:188). Legislation passed in 1994 sanctioned a mass privatization scheme based on vouchers similar to the Czech model. Voucher privatization was actually launched in 1995–96 (Todeva, 2000:187). One of the recurrent features of the Bulgarian experience of privatization has been the high degree of politicization (Bristow, 1996:199) and the discourse of privatization has been matched in reality only partially by the actual sale of state assets and corporate restructuring.

Jones and Nikolov (1997), in their study of 360 Bulgarian manufacturing firms, analysed data from the period 1989–92 in order to categorize firms as 'good', 'bad' or 'ugly'. 'Good' firms were defined as those with profits and low levels of indebtedness in 1992. 'Ugly' firms are those falling in the lowest two quintiles of profitability and with high levels of indebtedness, while all remaining firms were assigned to the category of 'bad' firms. As a result of the analysis 64 firms were defined as 'good', 209 as 'bad' and 87 as 'ugly'. The authors comment that the percentage of 'good' firms is considerably below the proportion of such firms in other CEE countries such as Hungary, Poland and the former Czechoslovakia. The authors also note the marked decline in employment and investment levels in the sample firms.

Interestingly, the slow pace of privatization has not been accompanied by a safeguarding of employment and job losses in Bulgaria have been particularly high. There is moreover no evidence that 'downsizing' is being driven by strategic considerations, as, apart from shedding labour, there appears to have been a slower pace of change in areas such as strategic behaviour. Furthermore, the scale of downsizing has contributed to a decline in organizational commitment on the part of employees, although this trend is partially compensated by a rise in declared work satisfaction (Ilieva, 1999).

Peev (1999) identified four types of firm in the Bulgaria of the late 1990s: non-transformed state-owned enterprises; corporatized enterprises (i.e. transformed but still in state hands and awaiting privatization); privatized enterprises with perverse behaviour; and privatized enterprises with market-oriented behaviour. A 'significant phenomenon of the privatization process, especially between 1992 and 1996, has been "wild crony" capitalism with a main network among former communist nomenclature circles, weak state institutions and the criminal world' (Peev, 1999:299).

Peev (1999) identifies both similarities and differences in behaviour and rationale between the different types of firm. For example, in the period 1992–94 there is evidence of both active and passive management, irrespective of type of company. In the subsequent period, however, that is 1995–96, there is evidence from company policies on investment and technology that privatization creates incentives for more efficient enterprise adjustment in the longer term. All types of enterprise, moreover, are involved in upgrading product quality, raising the standard of marketing and identifying new customers and markets. According to Peev (1999) the goals of the privatization strategy will be achieved only if there is further privatization (or reprivatization) and improved mechanisms of corporate governance.

Management after communism

The transition from the communist system of economic management undermined but did not transform the hierarchical and autocratic mode of management which had prevailed earlier. According to Michailova (1996:55) 'Management was extremely centralized, rigid, power motivated and not concerned with "human relations"', so that a 'them and us' attitude was widely encountered on the shop floor. There were, however, certain distinctions evolving between managers in state-owned enterprises and those in privatized firms (Todeva, 1996). While managers of state-owned enterprises had paid particular attention to the security and continuity of their activities, seeking to protect their own position and that of employees, the new private entrepreneurs as well as managers in privatized companies were more and more driven by the profit motive.

Attempts to make managers in the state sector more responsible and market oriented, after 1990 for example, by introducing open competitions for directorial positions were frustrated by the quality of the available pool of candidates and the way the competitions were actually conducted (Dimitrov, 1996; Estrin *et al.*, 1997). Moreover, because of the potential and actual power wielded by labour forces in the privatization process enterprise management in SOEs often sought to ensure that their decisions found a wide social acceptance (Todeva: 1996).

In the early 1990s therefore, Bulgarian management retained many autocratic features, reflecting not only communist practice but also a traditional Bulgarian characteristic of an inflexible attitude to power (Michailova, 1996). This was also the case in privatized companies where decision making remained highly centralized (Todeva, 1996).

This inflexible and authoritarian approach can be exemplified by managers' views and use of information (Michailova, 1996; Todeva, 1996; Koparanova, 1998). Formerly, information had been a source of power for party officials and was consequently monopolized by them. After the transition information became an additional source of power and status for managers, irrespective of company type. Todeva (1996:59) mentions in this respect 'non-democratic hidden mechanisms of controlled distribution of information among employees'. According to Koparanova (1998) the managing director determined the extent to which the researched company disclosed information to the general public and on occasions information was classified as confidential even though legally the public had a right to have it. An authoritarian management style can thus be accompanied by a certain degree of manipulation (Aaby *et al.*, 1997).

Management change in state-owned enterprises was also held back by other factors. In spite of demonopolization SOEs remained under state and ministry supervision and consequently the potential for managers developing their own discretion was limited. Furthermore, although demonopolization was intended among other things to encourage competition between firms, many managers preferred to rely on established networks of personal relations (Michailova, 1996; Michailova and Hollinshead, 1998).

Over time therefore distinctive types of managerial behaviour have evolved in Bulgarian companies (Todeva, 2000). While managers in state-owned companies have remained relatively passive and reserved, albeit becoming fairly adaptable, managers in privatized companies have tended to develop more entrepreneurial attitudes and modes of behaviour. In contrast to managers in the state-controlled sector they are more likely to be dynamic, proactive and risk-taking, although to a lesser degree than, for example, American managers (Aaby *et al.*, 1997). Aaby *et al.* found moreover that Bulgarian managers were subjected to a permanently high level of anxiety and stress.

These different managerial types, however, share numerous features in common as the new economic circumstances interplay with past practices in varying degrees. In their investigation of human resource management practices Michailova and Hollinshead (1998) comment with reference to the company to which they give the pseudonym of Kona that:

> Close scrutiny of Kona's approach to the management of employment reveals it to be a mosaic of policies, some of which were established in the previous era, sometimes masqueraded in a more modern guise, and others representing pragmatic adjustment to the new market situation.

The complexity of the situation in Bulgarian companies after 1990 is well illustrated by Reeves-Ellington's (1998) study, conducted in 1993–95, of the Rhodopski Kilim oriental carpet manufacturing cooperative in southern Bulgaria. The cooperative had survived under communism, in spite of the regime's monopolistic policies, because of the commitment of the director and the weaving supervisor. The latter was also the company's Communist Party secretary. After 1990 the cooperative needed to adapt rapidly to the new circumstances. The situation at the cooperative was complicated by the need to find markets, rejuvenate the workforce and deal sensitively with ethnic issues in an area with a mixed Bulgarian, Greek and Turkish population.

Numerous economic and cultural factors influenced the development of the cooperative. Bulgarians feel dominated by the external environment which can lead to feelings of being victimized and helpless. The cause of problems (and their solution) are related to external sources outside the control of the individual who consequently takes refuge in individual forms of response. Individualism in the private sphere thus goes hand in hand with public displays of collectivism. One of Reeves-Ellington's respondents explained the need for the individual to be independent of the environment in the following way:

> The Turks and then the Communists have taken each of us into their grasp and fashioned us. They were the supreme power. Both covered us with small, complicated rules, minute and uniform, in ways none of us could penetrate. We learned not to act but to avoid public actions. So we rebelled against these illegal controls in small and petty ways. We thumbed our noses at the state. (Reeves-Ellington, 1998:101)

Not surprisingly Bulgarians developed a high level of distrust towards the external environment and authority. This distrust is reflected in the reaction to offers of assistance which may be interpreted as an attempt to control the individual by placing him or her under an obligation to reciprocate.

In addition, there is a strong desire to avoid blame and thus many employees, especially older employees, express a preference for autocratic and highly structured human relations. This desire for the dominant, autocratic style of management is one way in which uncertainty can be avoided.

At the same time Reeves-Ellington noted that attitudes were evolving. For example, younger workers were less willing to accept the autocratic mode of management and expressed a preference for a more consultative and consensual style.

Conclusions

Against a background of weak institutional development and limited foreign direct investment and in an environment tolerating corruption and 'perverse' corporate behaviour, Bulgarian management has retained many of the features of the Soviet model of management introduced after the Second World War. An autocratic style is widespread and is moreover reinforced by traditional cultural values. Personal as much as market relationships influence company and manager behaviour. There is, however, some evidence of a change in expectations of managerial style, especially as younger managers indicate some preference for a more consultative and consensual approach.

References

Aaby, N-E., Marinov, M. and Marinova, S. (1997) 'Managers' Characteristics: Results from an Exploratory Comparison of Young Managers in Bulgaria and USA and its Implications for Management Education in Bulgaria', *Journal for East European Management Studies*, 2,1, pp. 22–34.

Bobeva, D. and Bozhkov, A. (1996) 'Foreign Investments in the Bulgarian Economy', in Zloch-Christy, I. (ed.), *Bulgaria in a Time of Change, Economic and Political Dimensions*, Aldershot: Avebury, pp. 119–31.

Bristow, A. (1996) *The Bulgarian Economy in Transition*, Cheltenham: Edward Elgar.

Crampton, R. (1997) *A Concise History of Bulgaria*, Cambridge: Cambridge University Press.

Dimitrov, M. (1996) 'Privatization: Its Goals, Progress to Date and Prospects', in Zloch-Christy, I. (ed.), *Bulgaria in a Time of Change, Economic and Political Dimensions*, Aldershot: Avebury, pp. 119–31.

Estrin, S., Dimitrov, M. and Richet, X. (1997) 'State Enterprise Restructuring in Bulgaria, Romania and Albania', *Discussion Paper No. 47*, London: LBS CIS-Middle Europe Centre.

EBRD (1998) *Annual Report 1997*, London: EBRD.

Ilieva, S. (1999) 'Work Attitudes in Transition: Some Implications for Management of Organizational Change in Bulgaria', *Journal for East European Management Studies*, 4,4, pp. 279–91.

Jones, D. and Nikolov, S. (1997) 'Enterprise Adjustment During Early Transition', in Jones, D. and Miller, J., *The Bulgarian Economy: Lessons from Reform during Early Transition*, Aldershot: Ashgate, pp. 249–71.

Koparanova, M. (1998) 'Danone-Serdika JS Co', *East European Economics*, 36,4, pp. 27–39.

Lavigne, M. (1999) *The Economics of Transition, From Socialist Economy to Market Economy*, Basingstoke and London: Macmillan, 2nd ed.

Michailova, S. (1996) 'Approaching the Macro-Micro Interface in Transitional Societies: Evidence from Bulgaria', *Journal for East European Management Studies*, 1,1, pp. 43–70.

Michailova, S. and Hollinshead, G. (1998) 'Developments in the Management of Human Resources in Eastern Europe – The Case of Bulgaria', *CEES Working Paper No. 9*, Copenhagen: Centre for East European Studies.

Peev, E. (1999) 'Ownership and Control Transformation and Discretionary Managerial Behaviour: The Case of Bulgaria', in Edwards, V. (ed.), Proceedings of the Fifth Annual Conference on *The Impact of Transformation on Individuals, Organizations, Society*, Chalfont St Giles: CREEB, vol. I, pp. 298–314.

Petrova, D., Pounds, N. and Pundeff, M. (1991) 'Bulgaria', in Bahr, L. and Johnston, B. (eds), *Collier's Encyclopaedia*, New York: Macmillan, pp. 696–718.

Reeves-Ellington, R. (1998) 'Cooperative Learning for Business Change: A Bulgarian Example', in Edwards, V. (ed.), Proceedings of the Fourth Annual Conference on *Convergence or Divergence: Aspirations and Reality in Central and Eastern Europe and Russia*, Chalfont St Giles: CREEB, pp. 94–114.

Todeva, E. (1996) 'Dynamics of Management Practices in Eastern Europe: The Case of Bulgaria', *Journal for East European Management Studies*, 1,4, pp. 47–63.
Todeva, E. (2000) 'Management in Bulgaria', in Warner, M. (ed.), *Regional Encyclopedia of Business & Management*, vol. 4: Management in Europe, pp. 184–92.

CHAPTER 8

Estonia

Although the smallest country discussed in this book Estonia is generally regarded as one of the success stories of the post-communist period. While the literature in English concerning Estonia is not extensive – some government publications, occupational reports and surveys by banks and accountancy firms, a handful of articles – the general tenor of this writing is positive, while recognizing that there have in the course of the 1990s been worries about inflation, bank crises, and employment. Like all the countries discussed in this book, the GDP of Estonia actually contracted in the first few years after the end of direct communism, which in the case of Estonia also meant the end of Russian control. Nonetheless, we will try to show that Estonia is reckoned to have done fairly well in terms of exports, FDI, close relationships with particular western countries, as well as in terms of economic stability and the emergence of a viable form of corporate governance. Estonia is also slated for first wave membership of the EU, alongside Poland, Hungary, the Czech Republic, and Slovenia – the small, rather prosperous state in the north-west corner of what used to be Yugoslavia. Estonia is the only one of the three Baltic States (Estonia, Latvia and Lithuania) that is 'first wave' scheduled. It may be helpful to start with a note on Estonia's history, which throws light on its current geo-economic position.

The past

A key feature of Central Europe is the disjunction between ethnicity and nationality (Lawrence, 1998). Ethnic groups, defined by language, that is to say have not been able to form themselves into discrete and enduring nation states. As we have seen in other chapters, all the countries in the region have had and still have ethnic minorities, and most of the countries have had a precarious and intermittent existence. So that Poland, for example, was partitioned out of exis-

103

tence by its three more powerful neighbours Austria, Prussia and Russia in the late eighteenth century, and not recreated as an independent state until 1918 at the end of the First World War. Then it was overrun by Nazi Germany in 1939, 'liberated' by the Soviet Union in 1944–45, and only freed itself from Russian domination in the 1980s. Or again, what we think of as Czechoslovakia was part of the Hapsburg Empire, again until the end of the First World War when a briefly independent Czechoslovakia was created, which in turn fell victim to Nazi Germany in 1938–39 and then to the Russians in 1945, and remained part of the Soviet Bloc until the Velvet Revolution of 1989.

Estonia has a past somewhat along these lines, except that for significant periods it has been dominated by Scandinavian countries. The Danes took the Estonian capital Tallinn in 1219, and for well over a hundred years it was under Danish influence until the Danes sold it to the Teutonic Order in 1343. The Livonian Wars (1558–83) between Sweden and Russia resulted in northern Estonia coming under Swedish rule and Southern Estonia coming under Polish rule. This state of affairs broadly lasted until the early eighteenth century when the Great Northern War (1700–21) between Peter the Great of Russia and Charles XII of Sweden resulted in a Russian victory, and a Russian occupation of both Estonia and Latvia that lasted until the First World War.

In the First World War (1914–18) Russia fought on the side of Britain, France and Italy, and against Germany and Austria-Hungary. But after the 1917 communist revolution Russia effectively dropped out and made a separate peace with its enemies. This was Estonia's chance.

On 24 February 1918 Estonia declared its independence, and fought against the German army until November 1918 when Germany surrendered to the Western Allies. Thereafter Estonia fought against Soviet forces until the Peace of Tostu in 1920. Estonia then enjoyed its first 20 years of independent statehood since the Middle Ages, until it was engulfed by the Second World War (1939–45). First it was annexed by the Russians in 1940, then overrun by Nazi Germany in 1941, 'liberated' by the Red Army in 1944 and re-incorporated into the Soviet Union until 1991. Russian troops pulled out in 1994. 24 February, the first occasion on which independence was declared back in 1918, remains Estonia's National Day.

There are some common threads in this story:

- Like much of the region, Estonia suffered from lying between two powerful countries, Russia and Germany.
- While some countries in Western Europe escaped the scourge of the First and Second World Wars, no country in Central Europe did.
- In common with the whole of Central Europe with the exception of the former state of Yugoslavia and Albania, it fell victim to the Soviet Union as the Red Army moved westwards in 1944–45 to close with its mortal enemy, Nazi Germany.
- Like the rest of the region, it finally emerged as an independent state

that lacked ethnic homogeneity, having a substantial Russian speaking minority.

But unlike the rest of Central Europe, because of its northern latitude and Baltic Coast, it also came under the influence of a variety of Baltic Powers – Denmark, Poland, Sweden – and continues to be affected by its Nordic proximity. It is a case of history being reinforced by geography, where Copenhagen is nearer to Estonia's capital Tallinn than is Moscow (523 miles as opposed to 540), Stockholm at 238 miles is only half the distance, and perhaps most significant of all Helsinki is only 52 miles away. Indeed there were regular ferry services between Tallinn and both Stockholm and Helsinki during the communist period, never mind afterwards. Tallinn has also traditionally been a city for Swedes and Finns to visit to have fun (booze and gambling) rather along the lines of Americans visiting Paris in the 1920s!

The Channel Isles?

Among outsiders there is a tendency to regard the Baltic States – Latvia, Estonia, and Lithuania – as a homogeneous group, rather like the Channel Isles!

But Estonia does differ from the others in a variety of ways. With a population of only 1.5 million it is the smallest, and only half the size of Lithuania. While something like a quarter of the population are Russian speaking, Estonian, unlike Lithuanian, Polish and Russian itself, is a Finno-Ugric language; that is to say it is related to Finnish and Hungarian (more closely to the first of these) not to the group of Slavonic languages predominant in Central and Eastern Europe. As we have seen, Estonia is distinguished by its links with Sweden and Finland, and Estonians like to boast that in the days of the First Republic their country had a higher GDP per capita than Finland itself.

One might also suggest that there is an element of Germanic, or at least German adoptions, to be found in Estonia. The predominant religious denomination is Lutheranism, as in the Protestant part of Germany (and in Sweden). Estonia used to be a member of the Hanseatic League, centred on the north German city of Lübeck. Estonia has now adopted a system of property law rather like the German system. Privatized Estonian public companies have two-tier boards – a non-executive supervisory board and an executive committee – just like German public companies. In post-communist Estonia all contracts of employment have to be in written form, cf. Germany (Lawrence, 1982) and every employee has to have such a contract including the managing director. The Estonian currency unit, the Kroon, is pegged to the Deutsche Mark at 8K:1DM.

Estonia has a somewhat unusual raw material – oil shale, and oil shale burning power stations. In the communist period some 20 per cent of all industrial workers were involved in oil shale production. Again during the communist period Estonia depended in part on its traditional industries and in part on the specialization ordained by the Soviet Union giving it an economic profile made up of chemicals, electronics, building materials, textiles, and wood-cutting/wood products. A lot of this has carried over into the post-communist period. A Price Waterhouse Coopers report claims Estonia now has traditional and a newly developed competitive advantage in wood, food processing, electronics, chemicals, textiles, energy and engineering (Price Waterhouse Coopers, 1998). Estonia's most important trading partner is Finland; a lot of industrial work in Estonia is in the form of sub-contracts from Finland, especially in electronics and telecommunications. Estonia is also distinguished from the other Baltic States by its relatively high credit ratings. As of end 1999 these stood at:

Moody's Investors Service	Baa
Standard & Poor's	BBB+
IBCA	BBB

Economic progress

By way of introduction it should be said that exporting to the West is not a new activity for Estonia, even if there have been interruptions. In the period 1918–20, when Estonia was still part of the Russian empire, it was one of the most industralized parts of that empire. In the period of the First Republic (1920–40) Estonia was already a significant exporter to the West. This western orientation was reactivated after the fall of communism, such that by 1994 some 70 per cent of Estonia's trade was with Western European countries and principally with the EU. By this time Estonia had a favourable trade balance with the UK.

Privatization

Underpinning this western orientation is the success of privatization in Estonia in the post-communist period. Before the fall of communism virtually the whole economy was owned by the Soviet state. But now the major part of the economy is in private hands, and this privatization is generally regarded as having been a success. The privatization includes the railways, the national airline, and gas. Readers might like to recall that railways were only privatized in Britain towards the end of John Major's period in office (1990–97) though Britain was not emerging from a fifty-year period as part of the Soviet Union! The telephone company and some power stations in Estonia remain to be privatized. Here again a western comparison may be relevant: it is only in the late 1990s that capitalist Germany has privatized the Deutsche Telekom, the national telephone provider.

This privatization has followed what might be called the German Treuhand model, where the Privatization Agency has enjoyed considerable freedom of manoeuvre to put state-owned enterprises (SOEs) up for sale, to negotiate with potential buyers, to organize public share offerings and public auctions. As a Price Waterhouse Coopers report on the Estonia economy (Price Waterhouse Coopers, 1998) puts it:

> Estonian privatization has now entered its final phase with only large-scale infrastructure companies left to be sold.

External trade

Returning to the theme of external trade there is strong patterning as to what Estonia exports, and as to the destination of these exports. Most important is that the export of machinery and equipment is in first place and accounts for something like 20 per cent of all exports in 1997. Clothing and footwear is in second place at 18 per cent of the total in the same year, and timber and paper production in third place at 16 per cent. Processed food comes next at 12 per cent, then chemicals at 6 per cent. There are some interesting differences in the destination of some of these principal exports. Most of the timber, for instance, goes to Sweden, Finland, Great Britain and Germany, while of the processed foodstuffs one third goes to Russia, while the Netherlands, Latvia and the Ukraine are next in order of importance.

Indeed it is also interesting to put the geographic origin and destination of imports side by side, percentage figures for 1997:

Exports		*Imports*	
21%	Finland	34%	Finland
18%	Sweden	10%	Sweden
10%	Russia	10%	Germany
9%	Latvia	8%	Russia
7%	Germany	38%	Others
3%	Lithuania		
30%	Others		

There are some simple but revealing points to be made here. First Finland and Sweden emerge as the top trading partners, a feature as we have argued of Estonia's history and geography, and to some extent of its linguistic and de-nominational alignment. Second there is strong two-way trade with Finland, Sweden, Russia and Germany, but with some asymmetry. Germany is clearly buying timber and other basic goods, while supplying (more of) the more sophisticated manufacturing goods characteristic of that country's economy (Simon, 1996). But with Russia it is the other way round, where Russia supplies energy and basic goods and takes processed foodstuffs and other manu-factured goods in return. Third, it is of note that neighbouring Latvia and Lithuania (the other 'Channel Isles') are significant export destinations, but Estonia imports rather less from them – an indication of Estonia's higher level of economic progress since the fall of communism. Finally, one might add that Estonia has functioned as a conduit for Russian trade with Western Europe, given its geographic position in central Europe and its Baltic Sea connections. This role however, is probably declining in importance since the earlier post-communist period, and has passed incrementally to Lithuania (though all parties to this movement of goods complain at the end of the twentieth century about the delays and inefficiencies on the Lithuanian-Polish border, probably gener-ated by Poland's irredentist claims against Lithuania.)

Sub-contracting

We have noted already that sub-contracting is at the end of the twentieth century a significant industrial activity in post-communist Estonia. The Estonian Ministry of Economic Affairs (1998:11) put the activity into context:

> As the majority of Estonian industrial enterprises do not have internationally known trademarks, their market relations are limited and there is a shortage of know-how and of money for research and development . . . sub-contracting has become one of the ways out. This ensures labour participa-tion, opens up Western markets, helps to improve the technical standing of production and labour culture, and introduces Western standards.

But there is a corresponding danger where sub-contracting work has a central role in a country's industrial activity, which is perceptively identified by the same source (The Estonian Ministry of Economic Affairs, 1998:11):

> The basic issue concerning the future is whether Estonian industry will be able to perform contract work so that it would remain competitive despite the rise in production costs, so that the earned profit, gained experience and skills and controls would enable, in a few years, to start more economical

performance of the same contract work, to start performing more complex and expensive operations, *to start producing their own products* (author's italics).

The message is clear. In the early days sub-contracting is 'nice work if you can get it', and for historical and other reasons Estonia is better placed to get it than some of its neighbours. But it cannot be an end state. There must be organizational learning and upgrading, know-how must lead to imitation.

Foreign direct investment

This is one of Estonia's key areas of achievement. Put baldly, in the period 1991–98 this tiny country attracted some FDI of US $1.8 billion, giving a per capita figure of US $700 over the whole period. This is a significant achievement, and puts Estonia ahead of all the CEE countries except Hungary (Hedman, 1998). If we take the sector breakdown for 1997 the picture that emerges puts manufacturing in first place:

37%	Manufacturing
21%	Wholesale and retail trade
16%	Financial services
12%	Transport and communications
6%	Real estate
8%	Other

The key change in the late 1990s was the rise in FDI in financial services, from 7.3 per cent of the total in 1996 to 16 per cent in 1997. There has also been a relative increase in investment in transport and communications.

In view of all that has been said the country origin of this FDI will come as no surprise. Again taking 1997 the figures were:

28%	Finland
21%	Sweden
7%	USA
6%	Russia
4%	Norway
34%	Other, widely distributed

While Finland is clearly dominant, its relative share has dropped by 5 per cent in the mid 1990s, and other countries including Norway, Denmark, and even Singapore are now 'in the frame'. This is probably to be regarded as a wholesome development. An over-dependence of one country upon another in economic life may well have consequences that are not sought: consider for example that 68 per cent of Canada's exports used to go to the USA; this has now risen to 80 per cent because of the North American Free Trade Agreement (NAFTA) but this economic dependence makes it difficult for Canada to maintain its cultural identity.

Aspects of management

The first point to make is that general writing about Estonia tends to distinguish it from Latvia and Lithuania in terms of temperament and mentality and to underline its Lutheran affiliation and relations with Nordic rather than with Slavonic countries. Even the casual visitor to Poland, for instance, can see what it is about the Poles that led them to win the Battle of Britain for us (depending on whose figures you believe, one in five or one in ten of the Battle of Britain pilots were Poles.) But the casual visitor to Estonia is more likely to be impressed by the reasonableness and measured seriousness of the people. This informs Estonian management style.

The second point is linguistic. There are some languages, such as Spanish, German and above all English, that are mastered by non-native speakers and used readily for business and operating purposes. This emphatically does not apply to Estonia! An impenetrable Finno-Ugric language, spoken by less than 1.5 million people is not likely to be mastered by other nationalities. The consequence of course is a rather high level of linguistic competence on the part of Estonian managers and others. Business visitors report widespread English-speaking ability, a knowledge of some German and even of Swedish is not uncommon; because of recent history (domination by the Soviet Union) as well as the minority of ethnic Russians referred to earlier, there is a considerable resource of Russian speakers, and Estonians are able to understand Finnish anyway.

A third feature that has shaped the character of Estonian management is the country's relative openness, notwithstanding the history of Russian domination. As already suggested this derives in part from location and traditional ties with Nordic countries, but also from relative size. Smallness does not automatically produce internationalism, but it often seems to facilitate it – recognized examples of this phenomenon in Western Europe would include Denmark, Holland and with some qualifications, Switzerland (Lawrence and Edwards, 2000). Or again in Eastern Europe smallness crossed with location seem to have produced the same result in the case of Slovenia (common borders with Western countries [Italy and Austria], widespread German speaking ability, Adriatic coastline, and so on).

A fascinating study that charts the development of Estonian management in the post-communist period is that of Kari Liuhto (1996). Liuhto is based at the

Turku School of Economics and Business Administration in Finland. Besides the general issue of post-communist economic and managerial transformation, Liuhto has a strong interest in FDI in Russia versus Estonia comparisons in the discussion of his research findings on Estonia.

This study is in the form of self-rating of managerial competence and development by a sample of Estonian managers, where they respond to twenty-five questions on managerial competence rating themselves on a seven point scale. More than this the study is longitudinal in that the subjects were tested on the eve of the disintegration of the Soviet Union in 1991, again in 1995, and were asked where they expected to be in 1999. While this is a study in self-reporting and therefore in self-assessment it is only fair to say that Estonians are not popularly given to euphoria or exaggeration, nor is the idea of *bella figura* (making a good impression, putting a good face on everything) dominant in Estonian society.

Findings from the study include the following:

- While Soviet management has been widely criticized for lack of business thinking, even back in 1991 Liuhto's sample did not see their business thinking as a conspicuous weakness.
- These Estonian managers were dissatisfied with their strategic planning in 1991; felt that there was a shortfall in control and realization of strategic plans in 1995, but not such as to endanger the progress of their enterprise.

On this last point Liuhto comments that: 'The answers given by the Estonian managers seem to suggest that management transformation has occurred faster than many Western experts were able to predict' (1996:13). Further evidence includes the findings that:

- the Estonian managers believed their commitment to objectives was already satisfactory in 1991,
- also that while the motivation of Estonian managers may be deficient, improvement has already occurred since 1991.

Liuhto sees this improvement as being the result of the competition between employing organizations (for managers) in turn driving a greater concern with Human Resource Management:

- Another interesting finding is that foreign companies operating in Estonia motivate these managers better than those in locally-owned companies.

It is not difficult, of course, to rationalize this finding *post factum*. Foreign (meaning Western) companies will have a greater perceived standing, and greater presumptive management know how; they are also likely to pay better, after the manner of US companies operating in Britain. But it is gratifying to be able to confirm this distinction on the basis of survey evidence. A further finding is that:

- in 1995 the Estonian managers rated time management as a key weakness.

It is unclear whether this is a feature of national culture or of poor infrastructure and lack of business services, and Liuhto canvasses both possibilities; but the managers anticipated improvement by the end of the 1990s:

- the Estonian managers in the survey felt in 1991 that decisions were planned better than strategies.

Again this is what one would expect at the end of the communist period, where 'companies' were really works, production units, and strategy formulation took place at government ministerial level (Edwards and Lawrence, 1994). As always the managers surveyed expected this gap between the quality of operational and strategic decision-making to narrow in the course of the decade:

- Liuhto notes that information hoarding was an accusation frequently levelled at Soviet managers, yet the Estonians sampled in 1991 did not regard this as a problem.
- Finally these Estonian managers believed their willingness to take risks had increased significantly since the end of the communist period.

In explaining this last point and some related findings Liuhto notes, quite rightly in our view, that in fact the Soviet economy 'demanded a lot of creativity as its business environment was in some turbulence, despite its stagnant facade' (1996:25). Summing up on the overall results of his longitudinal study Liuhto concludes:

> On the basis of the research data, one may suspect significant improvement in Estonian enterprise management. The areas which have advanced most rapidly are market-orientation, strategic management and cost-awareness (1996:27).

Of course the speed of the advance is partly explained by the low starting point and need to catch up. Yet Kari Liuhto's favourable judgement is consistent with some of the manifestations of economic progress reviewed in this chapter.

An open economy

No discussion of post-communist Estonia would be complete without drawing attention to the moves made by that state in the direction of an open economy. An investment act to encourage FDI was passed in 1991 immediately after the state's independence from Soviet Russia was secured. Similarly there are no limits on the imports or exports of foreign firms. All companies are allowed to have foreign currency accounts, and to maintain accounts with foreign banks. Estonia has also concluded treaties for the protection of investments with several foreign countries, including the USA, Britain and Germany, and of course with Sweden and Finland.

In 1995 Estonia concluded a free trade agreement with the EU. Estonia taxes the import of yachts and furs, and the export of cultural objets that pertain to the national heritage. Otherwise there is little in the way of tax restraints on import and export. Apart from the EU Estonia has also concluded free trade agreements with Latvia and Lithuania, with Slovakia, the Ukraine, the Czech Republic, with Turkey, and with what is left of EFTA. Estonia also has double taxation avoidance agreements with a range of countries. In 1996 the Tallinn stock exchange opened, and though it would be fair to say that it has had its ups and downs, it is the biggest among the Baltic States.

The relative speed and the comprehensiveness of this opening up of the economy are remarkable.

Corporate governance

Finally we might give some of the points raised in the previous section a further twist by pointing up their significance for corporate governance. Antti Ainamo and William Cardwell of the Helsinki School of Economics and Business Administration have considered the development of corporate governance in the Baltic States though in practice their focus is on Estonia (Ainamo and Cardwell, 1998). Their feisty definition of corporate governance is that it is 'the structure that keeps management from pursuing its own goals at the expense of owners and other stakeholders' (1998:136). These researchers note the developments and/or institutions that have been key to the emergence of a system of corporate governance in Estonia:

- the setting up of the Hansabank and its rapid establishment as the leading commercial bank in the Baltic States; it diversified at an early stage into investment banking, money management, real estate, and loans; in 1994 it was listed on the Helsinki stock exchange,
- the establishment of the Tallinn stock exchange in 1996, as already noted; a stock exchange provides a legitimate and controlled forum for the trading of corporate value – this in itself is unusual in economies in transition; and of course it helped to attract foreign investment,
- the 1995 Business Code, with provisions that broadly reflect western practice; it includes the provision for two-tier boards in public companies, noted earlier.

To put this into context it should be said that such regulation and stability are unusual in economies in transition, where the powerful grab corporate property and the absence of the rule of law frightens off would-be foreign investors. The absence of this kind of regulation has been a *leitmotiv* of the early post-communist period in Central and Eastern Europe, and no country has received more criticism in this respect than Estonia's former master – Russia. For Estonia it is not so much a case of small is beautiful, but small is orderly. And order is a *sine qua non* for economic development.

References

Ainamo, A. and Cardwell, W. (1998) 'After Privatization: Economic Development, Social Transformation and Corporate Governance in the Baltic States', *Journal for East European Management Studies*, 3, 2, pp. 134–163.

Edwards, V. and Lawrence, P. (1994) *Management Change in East Germany*, London: Routledge.

Hedman: Attorneys at Law (1998) *Estonian Business Law*, Tallinn, Estonia.

Lawrence, P. (1982) *Personnel Management in West Germany: Portrait of a Function*, (West) Berlin: International Institute of Management and Administration.

Lawrence, P. (1998) *Issues in European Business*, London and Basingstoke: Macmillan.

Lawrence, P. and Edwards, V. (2000) *Management in Western Europe*, London and Basingstoke: Macmillan.

Liuhto, K. (1996) 'Management Transformation in the Former Soviet Union – Estonian Managers Evaluate Past and Forthcoming Transition,' *Journal for East European Management Studies*, 1, 3, pp. 7–30.

Ministry of Economic Affairs (1998) *Estonian Economy 1997–1998*, Tallinn: Republic of Estonia.

Price Waterhouse Coopers (1998) *Economy*, Tallinn, Estonia: Estonian Investment Agency.

Simon, H. (1996) *Hidden Champions*, Boston, Mass.: Harvard Business School Press.

CHAPTER 9

Management in the countries of the former Yugoslavia

The development of management in the successor states of the former Yugoslav Federation has been strongly influenced by the respective states' historical, cultural and economic legacy as well as by their experience of the break-up of Yugoslavia since 1989 (Edwards, 2000).

Yugoslavia's existence as an independent state lasted for the period 1918–89. Prior to 1918 the various components of what became Yugoslavia were subjected to various foreign dominations. Slovenia and Croatia had previously formed part of the Austro-Hungarian Empire; since the establishment of the Dual Monarchy (Austria-Hungary) in 1867 Slovenia and Dalmatia (the latter now part of Croatia) were ruled from Vienna, while the main part of Croatia was ruled from Budapest. Most of the remaining parts of Yugoslavia had formed part of the Ottoman Empire, which in the nineteenth century was forced to relinquish its possessions in the Balkans to new independent states. One of the beneficiaries of Ottoman decline was Serbia which gained its complete independence from Ottoman rule in 1878. In 1918 Serbia and Montenegro united with these former parts of Austria-Hungary to form Yugoslavia.

The legacy of the various occupying powers was reflected in and combined with differing ethnic and religious dispositions. The Slovenes of north-eastern Yugoslavia and the Croats were predominantly Roman Catholic, the Serbs overwhelmingly Orthodox. In central and southern Yugoslavia there were substantial numbers of Muslims. In addition to being diverse from the point of view of religion, at the time of its foundation Yugoslavia also had substantial ethnic minorities: Albanians and Macedonians in the south and Germans and Hungarians in the north. The dividing line between ethnic and religious differences was moreover not always clear. Based on Wiskemann's figures (1966:268) Serbs,

Croats and Slovenes accounted for around 80 per cent of the population of Yugoslavia in the decade preceding World War II.

Events since 1989 have accentuated the differences between the various constituent republics of the former Yugoslav Federation. The Federation did not disappear completely but was soon reduced to Serbia and Montenegro only. The period since 1989 has furthermore been marked by a series of military conflicts which have seriously affected economic and social life across large parts of the country. In some instances conflict was of brief duration (as in the case of Slovenia). However, other conflicts as between Croatia and Serbia, in Bosnia-Hercegovina and over the Serbian province of Kosovo have been more protracted and bitter, involving in the last cited example NATO intervention in 1999. These conflicts have resulted in considerable bloodshed, hatred and distrust and have tended to detract from the task of establishing functioning political and economic systems to replace the Yugoslav model of socialism, which had been a hallmark of Yugoslavia for four decades from the 1950s to the 1980s.

The Yugoslav model of socialism

Numerous writers (for example Barratt Brown, 1984), have described and analysed the Yugoslav model of socialism. Interest in the Yugoslav experience was based both on the fact that it diverged from the Soviet model and that it offered an economic model for developing countries, particularly those that were politically aligned neither to the Soviet Union nor the USA (Zeffane, 1988). The key characteristics of the Yugoslav model were social ownership of property, decentralization of decision-making, self-government and self-management of economic enterprises.

By a constitutional law of January 1953, state ownership of property was transferred to the population. This law was applied to economic enterprises and other institutions such as hospitals. These organizations were now owned and managed by various local authorities on behalf of society as a whole.

Social ownership in combination with decentralization of governmental functions established a system which differed in substantial elements from the Soviet model which emphasized state ownership and control. Decentralization gave a key role for decision-making and implementation of organizational plans to local authorities and individual organizations.

With decentralized decision-making the national plan functioned as a coordinating framework for the activities of the totality of individual organizations. This aspect was fundamentally different from the Soviet model where the central plan was the starting point for the activities of individual enterprises which were each allocated production targets.

Decentralization was reinforced in the 1960s when 'ownership' of economic enterprises was transferred to the workers themselves. From the legal point of view nobody actually owned the enterprises, but in principle employees enjoyed the economic benefits of ownership. Furthermore in 1965, economic enterprises were opened up to world market forces as many import controls were removed. To a far greater degree than among the communist states of Central and Eastern Europe, Yugoslav economic enterprises were subjected to the competition of western companies and products and the free market system. A further dimension of the opening up of the Yugoslav economy was the permission given to Yugoslav workers to work abroad. Many were employed as guest workers (*Gastarbeiter*) in the Federal Republic of Germany. This latter practice benefited the Yugoslav economy in two ways: firstly it reduced the pressure on employment at home; secondly the remittances of the Yugoslav guest workers represented a valuable source of hard currency.

However, the aspect of the Yugoslav system of economic management which has possibly attracted most interest has been the concept of self-management as embodied in the worker-managed enterprise.

Self-management did not signify that workers managed the enterprise directly. In enterprises with at least 70 workers the total workforce elected a Workers' Council of at least 15 members. Members of the Workers' Council were elected for a two-year period, 50 per cent of members being renewed annually. The Workers' Council elected each year a Management Board as its executive body. The Management Board was then responsible for the appointment of the General Director of the enterprise and for the senior managers. Appointment was normally for a four-year period and renewable. The system of self-management in Yugoslavia differed fundamentally from the Soviet model as practised in other CEE countries, where industrial organizations were in general run on a consensual basis by a combination of enterprise management, the communist party and the trades union.

In the early 1970s there was a further development of the concept of self-management. The so-called Basic Organizations of Associated Labour (BOAL) were introduced and became the basic unit of economic organization, a function previously fulfilled by the enterprise (Petkov and Thirkell 1991:179). One aim of this change was to reduce the power of managers which had expanded as a result of the influence of market forces (Zeffane 1988:413). The enterprise could in consequence be considered a federation of BOAL.

Under self-management enterprises were involved in investment decisions, which were partly influenced by the overall plan as well as by the enterprise itself. Sources of investment funding could be either internal (by allocating part of the enterprise surplus to investment rather than wages and salaries) or external (by taking on bank loans). Interest rates for such loans were no more than nominal, never exceeding 6 per cent even when inflation began to soar.

As well as arousing considerable interest the Yugoslav model has received a number of criticisms. Barratt Brown (1984:65) describes the model as 'Utopian in its expectations'. In practice many workers were unwilling or ill-prepared to fulfil the role expected of them. Furthermore, the BOAL, as the basic unit of organization, tended to encourage the fragmentation of enterprises. The macro-economic benefits of self-management were also difficult to assess. While gross national product (GNP) had grown at an annual rate of 5.9 per cent in the 1960s and 5.4 per cent in the 1970s, this had declined to 1.2 per cent in the first half of the 1980s. Subsequently GNP actually declined in real terms. The 1980s were a decade of high and rising inflation and declining productivity. To quote Warner (1990:23): 'What had been designed as a consensual mechanism, albeit imposed from the top, began to reveal its structural weakness!'

In spite of its shortcomings the self-management system did have certain advantages with regard to management practice and development. Yugoslav enterprises, although extending a large degree of opportunity for participation in decision-making to employees, were in reality controlled overwhelmingly by top managers and specialists (Heller *et al.*, 1998:169). In many respects enterprise top management enjoyed a considerable degree of autonomy. Furthermore, a whole generation of Yugoslav managers were trained under self-management (Heller *et al.*, 1998:193). This experience was a far better basis for responding subsequently to the challenges of a market economy.

The collapse of Yugoslavia

In the early 1990s the Yugoslav Federation began to fall apart although this process was fiercely resisted by Serbia. Slovenia was the first of the Yugoslav republics to leave the Federation, declaring its independence in 1991. Subsequently other republics – Croatia, Macedonia and Bosnia-Hercegovina – also declared their independence. In the case of Croatia and Bosnia-Hercegovina secession was followed by intense warfare between competing ethnic groups. The case of Slovenia is, however, noteworthy because military conflict lasted a very short period of time and Slovenia was as a consequence able to focus on issues of economic and political transformation.

Slovenia

In the 1990s Slovenia emerged as one of the most economically advanced countries of CEE and a leading contender for EU membership. Economic statistics (Bates, 1999) portray Slovenia as by far the richest of the formerly socialist countries, with a gross domestic product per capita close to US$10 000 (a figure close to that of Portugal, the poorest of the current EU members). The CEE country closest to Slovenia in this respect is the Czech Republic with a per capita GDP below US$6000.

In spite of its small size (the population is approximately 2 million), Slovenia has also been considered an attractive location by foreign investors. Cumulative FDI-inflows per capita over the period 1989–97 have been the fourth highest in the region and in 1997 only Hungary attracted more FDI per capita (EBRD, 1998:17).

The situation in Slovenia since 1991 has been strongly influenced by the country's history, namely the centuries of Austrian rule from 1282 to 1918 and Slovenia's more recent history as a part of Yugoslavia (1918–91). Slovenia was for over six centuries part of the Hapsburg Empire and Slovenes are wont to refer to the working population's 'Germanic' work-related values. To many Slovenes Austria is a role model to be emulated and there is a strong identification with Austria on the part of many Slovenes. Austrian influence tends to be pervasive and diffuse and is, somewhat paradoxically, a marked element of Slovene identity.

Slovenia's participation in Yugoslavia has been of shorter but more recent duration. Consequently, its impact has been more explicit and direct. With the collapse of Yugoslavia Slovenia lost what had been the largest part of its domestic market. Slovene companies also lost control of assets they owned in other Yugoslav republics.

Moreover, the establishment (after 1945) of a communist regime in Yugoslavia, which pursued a distinctive path to communism, determined the way the economy and individual enterprises were organized.

The collapse of Yugoslavia has had a significant impact on the operation of the Slovene economy. By early 1992 sales to the former Yugoslav market had shrunk to below 30 per cent of their former level; additionally exports to Eastern Europe had fallen from 30 per cent of exports in 1985 to 12 per cent in 1991 (Bodenhöfer and Stanovnik, 1992).

Slovene companies after 1990

Case studies of Slovene companies in the early 1990s indicated that at least a small number had an international competitive advantage as defined by Porter (1990). One such company was Alpina (Ray, 1993) which manufactured sports and fashion boots. Alpina had 25 per cent of the world market for cross-country ski boots and 2–3 per cent of the world market for downhill ski boots. 80 per cent of sales were accounted for by exports, 90 per cent of which went to

Western Europe. Although affected by the loss of its retail outlets and plants in other ex Yugoslav republics, the company had been able to overcome these losses because of its strong export performance.

Another example is provided by Estrin and Richet (1996:20–21). Kolektor, a manufacturer of commutators, had had a cooperative agreement with a German company since the late 1960s. This agreement was subsequently taken over by an American company. Kolektor, however, under these agreements managed to retain a substantial freedom of action because of its level of technology and managerial expertise. Kolektor enjoyed considerable international recognition and exported over 80 per cent of its output.

Slovene managers in the early 1990s

Slovenia had been in the forefront of introducing western-style management development in central and eastern Europe with the establishment of the Brdo Management School in 1986 (Warner, 1990).

One survey (Bodenhöfer and Stanovnik, 1992) investigating how Austrian investors viewed the capabilities of Slovenian managers underlined the higher level of management abilities of Slovene managers, when compared to those of other communist economies and to those of managers in developing countries. A majority of respondents were of the opinion that most Slovene managers in Austrian direct investment projects were as capable as managers in the Austrian company. Reasons cited for the relative superiority of Slovenian managers compared to managers in other countries of Central and Eastern Europe included the tradition of decentralized decision making and 'market socialism' which gave managers in the former Yugoslavia greater independence and responsibility for managing and developing companies and for selling their products, in particular abroad.

Nevertheless a number of key weaknesses were also identified, for instance, knowledge of and competence in marketing, general management and financial management. In this respect Slovene managers demonstrated similar deficiencies to those of managers throughout CEE, though possibly to a lesser degree.

When interviewed in 1994 (Edwards and Lawrence, 1995), Slovenian managers commented that the nature of managerial work had changed with the demise of self-management. One manager commented that self-management had been 'beautiful for those who had wanted to just put their feet up'! Considerable managerial time had been expended in attending various boards and committees rather than on managerial activities themselves and the initial impetus that self-management had provided had soon dried up.

With the change of economic system managers consequently enjoyed a lower intensity of work as there was no longer a need to attend the numerous meetings associated with the process of self-management and they also enjoyed more discretion to exercise their managerial prerogative. However, managers also indicated that external pressures had increased and there was generally more pressure on them.

Many of the interviewees in the Edwards and Lawrence survey (1995) were managing directors or their deputies. The majority had held senior political office at the federal (i.e. Yugoslav) and/or republican (Slovene) level under the former regime. This was a further indication of the continuing influence of the Yugoslav dimension on the transition in Slovenia. Not only was identification with the former political system apparently not a bar to participation in the new economic system, but political experience of a high order under the former regime seemed to be regarded as a valuable attribute in the management of companies.

Privatization

The privatization debate in Slovenia was characterized by intense political debates. The privatization scheme eventually adopted was to say the least complex. The 1992 Law on Ownership Transformation sought to prevent 'wild privatizations'. It combined the issue of certificates to citizens who could then use them to buy shares in their own or any other company that also included within its privatization programme a public offering of shares or invest them through investment funds. Proportions of shares were also reserved for internal buyout or commercial privatization as well as for transfers to the Pension Fund and the Compensation Fund (Böhm and Simoneti, 1993).

The privatization scheme clearly acknowledged the former concept of social ownership through the issue of certificates and the provision for management and employee buyouts (MEBOs). One outcome of the Slovenian approach has been the relatively high number of MEBOs. However, the high incidence of insider-owned firms does not appear to have been a serious impediment to the development and growth of the Slovenian economy. Nevertheless, concerns have been expressed about the continuing high involvement of the state in the Slovenian economy (estimated at around 50 per cent of GDP) and the widespread existence of MEBOs. These two factors have been regarded as being detrimental to the development of an effective system of corporate governance (*Wirschaftslage und Reformprozesse in Mittel- und Osteuropa*, 1999:88).

By the end of 1997, 1329 social (state) enterprises had been privatized (there had been around 3400 such enterprises prior to the start of the transition at the end of the 1980s). More than three quarters of these privatized enterprises now have predominantly internal owners, with less than one quarter having predominantly external owners. Privatization created a huge number of shareholders, but a process of ownership concentration seems to have rapidly decreased their number by one third. What is evident is that the process of privatization and restructuring has been strongly influenced by the legacy of workers' self-management (Pučko and Edwards, 1999).

Enterprise restructuring in Slovenia

Pučko *et al.* (Pučko and Lahovnik, 1997a; Pučko and Lahovnik, 1997b; Pučko, 1999; Pučko and Edwards, 1999) have identified three distinct phases in the restructuring process of Slovenian enterprises since 1990. The first phase (1990–93) was characterized by enterprise retrenchment which adversely affected output and the size of the workforce. The main characteristics of the second phase (1994–mid 1997) were linked to a certain hiatus in enterprises' strategic restructuring and a preoccupation with enterprise privatization activities. The third phase covers the period since mid 1997 in which privatized enterprises began to pay greater attention to factors of total quality management though they were not yet able to integrate them comprehensively in their business operations.

During the first transformational phase top managers in enterprises dealt mostly with key issues such as formulating a new strategy for the enterprise, recruiting and developing staff to meet the need for managerial and professional human resources, reducing the labour force, reducing cost levels, coming to grips with renewing the enterprise's product range, finding new markets and introducing organizational changes.

The second transformational phase required top managers to dedicate most of their time to the firm's privatization, market development, cost reduction, training and skills development, product quality improvement, building new strategic partnerships and company reorganization.

In the third phase issues of total quality management became central. These included management quality, flexibility, reliability of deliveries, product quality, employees' skills and knowledge, creativity and innovation, the firm's reputation, firm growth and therefore the overall enterprise culture. These issues now became the focus of top managers' endeavours.

As a consequence of the restructuring process the majority of 'old' Slovenian enterprises seem to be performing satisfactorily again, with less than 10 per cent of firms still experiencing some kind of crisis, although around 20 per cent of the firms have still to complete their strategic restructuring. In addition, somewhat more than 10 per cent of the enterprises may still have to face bankruptcy in the foreseeable future. Nevertheless, by 1998, privatized enterprises in Slovenia, irrespective of the degree of external and internal ownership, were reporting, according to statistics quoted in Pučko and Edwards (1999:85), a rising level of return on equity.

Management transformation in Slovenia

Pučko (1999) in a survey conducted in 1997–98 found that the typical 'old' Slovenian enterprise was run by a top management team consisting of ten members. Over two thirds of them had a university degree. Their age distribution indicated that a significant proportion of the former socialist top managers had taken early retirement. This fact explains why fewer than 10 per cent of the top managers are more than 56 years of age. In a 1996 survey Pučko and Lahovnik (1997a) found that fewer than 10 per cent of managing directors were in this age bracket. The majority of top managers are therefore relatively young, with 41 per cent in the age bracket of between 36 and 45 years. Top managers have on average 20 years of overall work experience and 14 years of experience in their present company.

With this age profile Slovenian top managers are more likely to display evidence of creativity, a long time horizon and an attitude of taking on any necessary business risk. Furthermore, around three quarters of top managers had held their current or a similar position for the previous five years, indicating increasing stability in the composition of top management teams and a stabilization of the process of managerial regeneration.

There is evidence of a new class of Slovenian top managers who have a stake in the market economy which the country has been developing in the 1990s. These new managers still share the same traditions and are subjected to the same environment as old managers, but a significant number of younger managers 'do not carry the baggage' (Vlachoutsicos, 1999:492), do not identify with the managerial values and practices of the previous socialist self-management economy and understand increasingly well the challenges and constraints of the market economy.

Slovenian managers' values have been changing slowly though significantly during the transition period. They still differed noticeably from the value systems of Western European entrepreneurs and managers in the second phase of enterprise restructuring. For example, Slovenian top managers were much more inclined to internationalize their firm's operations than their Western European counterparts (Pučko and Lahovnik, 1997a:364). A striving for profit maximization is also a value on which Slovenian top managers place much more emphasis than their colleagues in the West. These empirical research findings indicate the marked openness to change of Slovenian managers.

On the other hand the personal objectives of the managing directors of 'old'

Slovenian enterprises appear well aligned with the personal objectives of West European entrepreneurs and managers. Personal financial independence and better personal performance seem to be more important for Slovenian managers than for their West European counterparts. Otherwise both groups of managers attach very little importance to factors that are primarily socially oriented (Pučko and Lahovnik, 1997a:368–369). Profit sharing also appears to be a value which is appreciated much more by Slovenian managers than by their West European counterparts. Attitudes towards maintaining good work conditions, saving jobs, improving their employees' life style, participation of employees in ownership and decision-making are already very similar or even identical to those held by managers in Western Europe.

Developments in other former Yugoslav republics

The situation in other parts of the former Yugoslavia has developed very differently from that prevailing in Slovenia. Even taking into account the fact that Slovenia had been the most economically advanced and prosperous of the former Yugoslav republics, the gap with the other countries has increased, to a large extent because of the lack of peace and stability in these countries. This gap can be illustrated from data on GDP per head (*Wirtschaftslage und Reformprozesse in Mittel- und Osteuropa*, 1999: various pages).

	GDP per head 1998 (US$)
Slovenia	9899
Croatia	4500
Bosnia-Hercegovina	2034
FYR Macedonia	1800
Yugoslavia (i.e. Serbia and Montenegro)	1455 (1997)

The gap is also reflected in the statistics for FDI (EBRD, 1998:17). Over the period 1989–97 Slovenia attracted US$543 per head, Croatia US$233 and Macedonia US$31. The gap between Slovenia and Croatia has, however, been narrowing. In 1997 Slovenia attracted US$170 per head, Croatia US$105 and Macedonia US$8.

Compared to Slovenia the other countries of the former Yugoslav Federation have lagged behind considerably in the transformation process and are now attempting to catch up as speedily as possible on lost time. For instance, since the cessation of hostilities with Serbia the privatization process in Croatia has been accelerated.

The former Yugoslav republic which has endured most from the suffering and bloodshed following the collapse of Yugoslavia has been Bosnia-Hercegovina. The estimated war damage in Bosnia is in the region of US$20 billion, GDP was reduced to a quarter and industrial output to around 10–15 per cent of their pre-war level. In addition, Bosnia was faced with a gigantic trade deficit as the collapse of domestic production resulted in the importation of many products (Buchan, 1998a:I). Moreover, following the end of the war, companies have been faced with an environment which has changed considerably. Established enterprises accustomed to supplying primarily the former Yugoslav market are now confronted with a number of smaller, more fragmented markets. The Zenica steel works, for example, which is located to the north-west of the Bosnian capital Sarajevo has had to endure massive cutbacks in output and manpower. Output has fallen to 100 000 tonnes a year, with employment dropping from 25 000 to under 5000 (Buchan, 1998b:V).

Since the end of the conflict in 1995, Bosnia-Hercegovina has experienced some return to stability and spectacular growth rates which, however, have to be interpreted in the light of the devastation wreaked by the period of intense warfare. Understandably, under such circumstances, management has largely been pre-occupied with day-to-day crisis management.

In Croatia too, economic restructuring was held back by military conflict. Although Croatia decided on a path similar to Slovenia's with regard to privatization, the Croatian privatization process developed relatively more slowly and was possibly subject to greater government control. One reason for this was the Croatian government's desire to use the proceeds from the sale of state enterprises to finance unemployment and reconstruction (Bartlett and Bateman, 1997).

The process of economic transformation was also boosted by an expansion of the small business sector, particularly in trade, financial and business services (Bartlett and Bateman, 1997). This expansion had redressed not only the structural imbalance of the former Yugoslav economy, with its preference for large enterprises but has also created a substantial group of business people who own and run their own companies and are personally committed to the market reforms.

Conclusions

The former Yugoslavia was characterized by cultural, ethnic and economic diversity. The differences between the successor states are likely to persist, with diversity increasingly reinforcing divergence. The former economic system created a certain homogeneity of approach in the individual republics of the Federation. Now that the Federation has to all intents and purposes disappeared, two main lines of development seem to be emerging with regard to management evolution.

Slovenia and Croatia are strongly oriented to West European values and affiliations. Slovenia is one of a first group of CEE countries to be offered admission to the European Union (EU), while Croatia is regarded as a possible candidate for a second group of EU aspirants, provided that it succeeds in establishing democratic institutions acceptable to existing EU members. Management in both Croatia and Slovenia therefore will become more integrated in West European approaches and practices. In view of both countries' historical legacies and current aspirations, the development of Croatian and Slovenian management is likely to tend towards practice in Germany and Austria.

The situation in the other successor states of former Yugoslavia is more difficult to ascertain. The future of these countries appears more uncertain because of general political instability and relative poverty. The respective legacies of the Orthodox Church and Ottoman rule would suggest, however, that management would tend to be autocratic (Hickson and Pugh, 1995:134). While the Orthodox legacy will continue to be influential in Serbia and Montenegro, Islamic influences are likely to assert themselves in Bosnia-Hercegovina and the province of Kosovo, especially if economic reconstruction and regeneration receive significant support from other Islamic countries. The precise development of FYR Macedonia is more difficult to predict because of its complex ethnic (Macedonian, Albanian, Serb) and religious (Orthodox, Muslim) composition.

Somewhat paradoxically, the legacy of self-management will persist, albeit diluted in the form of codetermination translated from German practice, to a greater extent in Croatia and Slovenia than in the other successor states of Yugoslavia which hitherto have made less progress from the structures and practices of the former socialist federation.

References

Barratt Brown, M. (1984) *Models in Political Economy*, London: Penguin.

Bartlett, W. and Bateman, M. (1997) 'The Business Culture in Croatia and Slovenia', in Bateman, M. (ed.) *Business Cultures in Central & Eastern Europe*, Oxford: Butterworth-Heinemann, pp. 88–127.

Bates, S. (1999) 'Clubbed Together', *The Guardian*, 29 June.

Bodenhöfer, H.-J. and Stanovnik, P. (eds) (1992) *Wirtschaftsreform in Slowenien und Wirtschaftskooperation Slowenien-Österreich*, Klagenfurt and Ljubljana.

Böhm, A. and Simoneti, M. (eds) (1993) *Privatization in Central and Eastern Europe 1992*, Ljubljana: CEEPN.

Buchan, D. (1998a) 'Industry', in Bosnia-Hercegovina, *Financial Times Survey*, 21 October, p. V.

Buchan, D. (1998b) 'Trappings of a Fragile Statehood', in Bosnia-Hercegovina, *Financial Times Survey*, 21 October, p. I.

EBRD (1998) *Annual Report 1997*, London: EBRD.

Edwards, V. (2000) 'Management in the Former Yugoslavia', in Warner, M. (ed.) *The Regional Encyclopedia of Business & Management: Management in Europe*, London: Business Press, pp. 390–97.

Edwards, V. and Lawrence, P. (1995) 'The Transition to Capitalism in Slovenia', Chalfont St Giles: Buckinghamshire Business School Research Paper 3/95.

Estrin, S. and Richet, X. (1996) 'A Comparison of Foreign Direct Investment in Bulgaria, the Czech Republic and Slovenia', *Discussion Paper Series Number 49*, London: LBS CIS-Middle Europe Centre.

Heller, F., Pusic, E., Strauss, G. and Wilpert, B. (1998) *Organizational Participation, Myth and Reality*, Oxford: Oxford University Press.

Hickson, D. and Pugh, D. (1995) *Management Worldwide*, London: Penguin.

Petkov, K. and Thirkell, J. (1991) *Labour Relations in Eastern Europe, Organisational Design and Dynamics*, London and New York: Routledge.

Porter, M. (1990) *The Competitive Advantage of Nations*, New York: The Free Press.

Pučko, D. (1999) 'Transformation of the "Old" Slovenian Enterprises – Strategic Management View', in Edwards, V. (ed.) Proceedings of the Fifth Annual Conference on *The Impact of Transformation on Individuals, Organizations, Society*, Chalfont St Giles: Centre for Research into East European Business (CREEB), pp. 117–33.

Pučko, D. and Edwards, V. (1999) 'The Restructuring of Slovenian Enterprises in the 1990s – Views from Two Sides', *Economic and Business Review for Central and South-Eastern Europe*, 1, 1–2, pp. 67–89.

Pučko, D. and Lahovnik, M. (1997a) 'Managers in the Transformation Process of Eastern Europe – A Case of Slovenia', *Journal for East European Management Studies*, 2, 4, pp. 360–76.

Pučko, D. and Lahovnik, M. (1997b) 'Strategic Restructuring of Enterprises in the Transition Period: The Case of Slovenian Enterprises', *Management*, 2, 2, pp. 43–56.

Ray, P. (1993) 'Valuation of Firms in the Context of Privatization – Case: the Alpina Shoe Factory', Ljubljana: unpublished master's degree dissertation.

Vlachoutsicos, C. (1999) 'Internal Barriers to the Transition of Enterprises From Central Plan to Market', Proceedings of the Third Annual Conference on *Enterprise in Transition*, Split: Faculty of Economics, pp. 471–505.

Warner, M. (1990) 'Management Versus Self-management in Yugoslavia', *Journal of General Management*, 16, 2, pp. 20–38.

Wirtschaftslage und Reformprozesse in Mittel- und Osteuropa (1999) Berlin: Bundesministerium für Wirtschaft und Technologie.

Wiskemann, E. (1966) *Europe of the Dictators 1919–1945*, London: Collins.

Zeffane, R. (1988) 'Participative Management in Centrally Planned Economies: Algeria and Yugoslavia', *Organization Studies*, 9: pp. 393–422.

Past, present and future

Managers in the countries of Central and Eastern Europe (CEE) and the Former Soviet Union (FSU) have experienced considerable changes since 1989. During the 1990s managers in these countries had to come to terms with the consequences of system change in the political, social and economic spheres. In spite of the shock of this system change managers as a distinct category of individuals have been among the beneficiaries of the considerable transformation and upheaval which have taken place in the former communist states of the region. In general under communism it was the worker who was regarded as the ideal archetype of the socialist individual. Many of the communist countries styled themselves as workers' states and the ruling communist parties as workers' parties. In such circumstances, whatever the reality, managers were frequently denigrated and regarded almost as merely necessary and parasitical evils in the idealized transition process from the contemporary socialist society to the future communist Utopia.

The perception and area of competence of managers were also constrained by a range of other factors, in particular the structure and functioning of the command economy. Economies in CEE and the FSU were on the whole structured in such a way that managers possessed only limited discretion, as economic decisions at enterprise level were subordinated to plan guidelines and targets. Initiative did exist but tended to be limited to ensuring plan fulfilment.

In spite of the straitjacket of the Soviet model there was nonetheless some scope for variations between individual countries and opportunity for a greater degree of deviation in countries such as Yugoslavia which developed its own system of economic management. This diversity can be illustrated by reference to Kiezun's (1991) study of six CEE countries: Bulgaria, Czechoslovakia, East Germany, Hungary, Poland and Romania. Kiezun identified high levels of autocracy, bureaucracy and centralization in all six countries, although there was some variation in the degree of intensity of each of these factors. While the management style was described as autocratic in all the countries of the survey, in Czechoslovakia and East Germany this autocratic management style was mitigated by the self-discipline of the workforce, a reflection of both countries' pre-communist industrial traditions, while in Hungary and Poland the management style was distinctly less autocratic than in the other four countries. Moreover, organization in all six countries tended to be bureaucratic, with high degrees of bureaucracy in Czechoslovakia and East Germany and lower than average degrees of bureaucracy in Hungary and Poland. Similarly, all countries were highly centralized. Centralization was most evident in Bulgaria and Romania, less so in Czechoslovakia and East Germany, while Hungary and Poland had permitted some elements of decentralization.

There is, however, no easy correlation between these typical features of the command economy and actual economic performance. Productivity in Czecho-slovakia and East Germany tended to be high, with performance in Hungary and Poland generally superior to that of Bulgaria and Romania. Worker productivity was clearly influenced by a range of factors including the individual country's industrial tradition and the degree of self-discipline of the workforce. This tended to be high in Czechoslovakia and East Germany and only average in Bulgaria, Poland and Romania, with Hungary placed somewhere in between.

Kiezun's (1991) analysis provides us with an insight into the diversity of the countries of CEE and their different starting points after 1989. High levels of autocracy, bureaucracy and centralization were unlikely to inculcate the attitudes and behaviours required for the effective practice of management in a market economy. Unfortunately high levels of autocracy, bureaucracy and centralization often went hand in hand with extreme forms of distorted economic structures as, for example, in Bulgaria and Romania.

Drivers of change

A number of factors have accelerated the process of managerial transformation and regeneration within the overall context of the political and economic changes. First, privatization has altered fundamentally the relationships between all those involved in economic activities, from managers and workers to owners and consumers and also the state. Privatization has not only reallocated economic assets but has brought issues of efficiency, productivity and profitability to the fore. Managers, from being largely executors of superiors' decisions, are now more and more having to take the decisions themselves. Party discipline, moreover, is giving way to comparisons with competitors' performance and scrutiny by shareholders.

Second, the general opening of markets to foreign competitors and foreign direct investment have widened the opportunities for comparison with foreign companies and managers and have permitted the study, adoption and adaption of foreign ideas and practices. The influence of foreign ideas and practices has been particularly marked in companies which have been acquired by or have entered into joint ventures with foreign firms. In reality throughout CEE American and German firms have been particularly active in acquisitions and general commercial activity although firms from other West European countries, Japan and South-East Asia are also represented. American business ideas have also been influential through the medium of education and training, with many universities in CEE adopting American methods of teaching in business and management.

A third driver of change has been managers' own desire to establish and assert themselves as competent and valid managers. While certain managers were unable to come to terms with the consequences of the system change and went into retirement, many other managers seized the opportunity of being able to demonstrate their managerial knowledge and skills. Often there was an element of national pride in this, especially with the arrival on the scene of numerous foreign managers with proven experience of operating in market economies. Many managers in CEE initially underestimated the magnitude of the task facing them: it was not easy to acquire the knowledge, skills and practice which experienced Western managers had. However, many of these managers displayed enormous enthusiasm, desire to learn and compete as well as commitment to their companies many of which were experiencing considerable difficulties and required substantial surgery.

Managers now also enjoyed considerable benefits compared to the past and these benefits included status, prestige and financial rewards. In many cases managers are now able not only to assert the so-called managerial prerogative but are also the owners of company assets. As a result of the system change managers have thus been able to gain tangible as well as intangible rewards.

Barriers to change

The process of change has been by no means smooth and all countries have experienced substantial shocks in economic activity, employment, income and overall prosperity. While the need to privatize formerly state-owned assets is generally accepted, the pace of privatization has varied from country to country. Individual countries were understandably concerned to implement their privatization programmes in a way which would be economically beneficial to the future development of their countries and would not have excessive negative short-term impacts. These conditions and terms, however, permit a wide scope for interpretation as evidenced by the debates relating to gradualism and shock therapy. Once again there is no obvious correlation between speed of privatization and economic recovery, as post-1989 economic restructuring has been influenced by a large number of variables.

Nevertheless, the recovery process has not been helped by political inertia and instability in some of the countries and there has been considerable debate about the persistence and role of former communist elites. What is worthy of note is that former communists have overwhelmingly accepted that the system change is irreversible and have committed themselves to working within the new system (many commentators have remarked that former communists have been in the best position to take advantage of the system change and have actually done so). Nonetheless, one decade after the collapse of the communist regimes, the economies of CEE and Russia are predominantly privately-owned economies, driven by private companies and entrepreneurs, with the outlook for companies still in state hands looking on the whole increasingly bleak.

Change, moreover, has been held back by the persistence of old practices and the emergence in some countries of widespread corruption and criminal activity. It would be argued that such phenomena are a consequence of the disappearance of the strong hand of communist rule, including autocratic rule, centralization and the widespread use of repression. This is a partial answer and these phenomena depend as much on the survival of communist and pre-communist attitudes and modes of behaviour as well as on the absence or weakness of effective state structures and social and individual codes of conduct. In some instances communism reinforced traditional practices which as a consequence are particularly difficult to eradicate.

Evolution of managerial cultures

It is in no way surprising that the system change has contributed to an evolution of management cultures. It is not, however, easy to pinpoint or generalize about the nature of this change. Whilst one could argue that all countries in the region have been affected by the previously discussed drivers of and barriers to change, the manner in and degree to which various factors have influenced developments in various countries have been highly varied. The overall impact of these factors has consequently also been subject to considerable variability. In general, there is a greater stress on individual rather than collective responsibility, on strategic rather than on predominantly operational decision-making. What is moreover clear is that organizational and managerial cultures are subject to enormous pressures for change, resulting not only from the collapse of communism, but also, as in the case of previously non-communist economies from factors such as globalization and regional economic integration (Lawrence, 1998).

National distinctiveness

In the preceding chapters we have largely argued that individual countries have their own distinctive management culture. Even with the superimposition of the Soviet model national differences persisted and as Kiezun's (1991) study indicated manifested themselves in the way the Soviet model was implemented and how it performed.

In 1996/97 the first-named author of this book organized a questionnaire survey of managers' attitudes to business and management in seven countries of Central and Eastern Europe: Croatia, the Czech Republic, Estonia, Hungary, Poland, Romania and Slovenia. The overall aim of the study was two-fold. Firstly, it was intended to identify the broad contours of the views of managements in countries in the region in order to assess the extent to which current views had evolved from those held under the former system of economic management. Secondly, the study also had the aim of identifying any differences in attitudes between managers in the respective countries. The overall picture of a Central/East European manager might thus be nuanced by the identification of distinctive national features.

The questionnaire was administered to managers attending management courses at universities in the respective countries. The respondents may thus be regarded as representing the more open and forward-looking contingent of managers in CEE. The questionnaire adopted had already been tested in Western Europe and North America in the context of the Loughborough studies (Lawrence and Edwards, 2000:117). The questionnaire collected a range of personal data on the respondents as well as their response to 86 statements relating to a number of business and management issues such as nature of management work, management qualities, hierarchy, decision-making and work and leisure. The questionnaire was structured using a five-point Likert scale.

The questionnaire was administered by local contacts in each country to a convenience sample of managers. In the case of Poland and Romania, the largest countries in the survey as far as population is concerned, two local contacts were involved in different localities.

The average age of the managers was just over 41. The Hungarian managers were on average the youngest group with an average age of just under 33, while the Estonian managers, with an average age of just over 44, were the oldest group. The clear majority of respondents were male. The managers, moreover, had varying lengths of service and experience as managers and filled at the time of the survey a range of general and functional management positions.

Following statistical analysis, the variables were examined to identify those with the highest mean, those with the lowest mean, a 'central' group of variables (i.e. those with a mean score which indicated neither agreement nor disagreement with the proposition), variables which displayed statistically significant differences between countries and variables with large standard deviations. As a result of this sifting procedure 37 variables were selected for further evaluation.

The 37 variables were then examined for thematic correspondence and grouped into seven groups, four major and three minor. The major groups comprised between five and eight variables, with the minor groups comprising only two variables. The main themes identified related to the nature of management, strategy and structure, work colleagues (both superiors and subordinates) and ethics. Minor themes were education, informal contacts and the relationship between work and leisure.

Major themes

Respondents projected a shared view of management as an activity which comprises decision-making as the central managerial act and now requires more judgement and discretion than under the former system. In the contemporary turbulent business environment management was above all concerned with the management of change. Senior managers, moreover, were regarded as primarily concerned with strategic issues.

Respondents, moreover, did not regard management and leadership as synonymous, with the Croat managers indicating the highest level of disagreement with this proposition. When asked about the *practice* of management respondents were in general (except for the Croat managers) less emphatic in identifying decision-making as the predominant activity, recognizing other dimensions of managerial work such as managing situations.

Two questions elicited a wide variety of responses. First, the proposition that 'management work is essentially about "fire-fighting" and removing "road blocks"' found general agreement among Croat, Czech and Romanian managers, while Estonian, Hungarian and Polish managers tended to disagree with the proposition (Slovenian managers were very much in the middle range of responses). These responses probably reflect the degree of transformation of the respective economies and the extent of progress towards market-economy patterns of behaviour. Managers in Croatia, the Czech Republic and Romania seem to be still stuck in the mould of the command economy in which managerial activity was concerned largely with resolving operational difficulties. Managers in the other four countries on the other hand appear to have moved on from such a position. Second, the proposition 'innovation and risk-taking is the preserve of senior management' was supported by the Czech and Estonian managers, while managers from the other countries tended to disagree, with the Polish managers disagreeing most strongly. These responses may reflect the contrast between more collectivist and individualist cultures as well as the permanence in some countries of attitudes and patterns of behaviour developed under communism. Certainly, the response of the Polish managers reflects the marked individualism of Polish culture.

Managers, especially senior managers were thus perceived as strategic decision makers, displaying judgement and discretion, responding to the challenges of environmental and organizational change. Issues relating to the day-to-day practice of management, however, reflected a range of opinions.

As already noted managers recognize the importance of strategy. In responding to three further propositions relating to relationships with customers and managerial motivation and promotion there was widespread (but not unanimous) agreement on the significance of building long-term relationships and a recognition that managers were not motivated solely by short-term considerations. Only in the case of the Croat managers was there a view that managers' decisions were primarily motivated by the desire to achieve short-term results and that the achievement of short-term financial targets was the main criterion for promotion. This may reflect the particular experience of economic transformation in Croatia which has been held back by the conflicts in the former Yugoslavia. The difficult and uncertain political environment is likely to have promoted among managers the need for short-term responses and overall a limited time horizon because of future uncertainty.

The propositions relating to the structure of organizations elicited a range of responses. There was general agreement that a company's structure may well change as the company's strategy changes (the Croat managers agreed most strongly, the Romanians least so, with the difference between the two groups statistically significant). As we concluded in chapter 6 on Romania, Romanian managers have tended to persist with the old ways of management, even in organizations perceived as successful. The proposition that 'structure is important in showing the relationship between the posts/functions/departments of the organization' found general agreement among the respondents, with the Croats, Estonians, Poles and Romanians most emphatic and the Czechs least so (the difference in emphasis being statistically significant). The responses of the Czech managers possibly indicate the slow pace of enterprise restructuring and management transformation in the country, as discussed in chapter 5. The proposition that 'a firm's formal communications systems are designed primarily to impart information downwards' received a mixed response, although Slovenian managers disagreed most and Romanians least. These responses reflect a number of issues relating to national management style (for example, degree of authoritarianism) and the extent to which companies in the respective countries have evolved from the archetypal state-owned enterprise of CEE.

A further proposition relating to the greater effectiveness of informal over formal systems in providing feedback on managers' performance was strongly rejected by Estonian and Polish managers and least rejected by Croat managers (with the difference being statistically significant). Such a response may reflect the extent to which traditional, 'personal' systems have given way to more formal, 'objective' systems of feedback in the respective countries. In Poland, for example, formal American systems and practices have been widely disseminated and implemented, even if with some resistance on the part of some local managers and employees.

While all but the Croat managers supported the long-term dimension of managerial activity, responses to issues of structure engendered a range of responses, reflecting significant differences in the way managers in the different countries perceive the function and effectiveness of various structural aspects of the organization.

Respondents project an image of collegial, supportive and cooperative relationships among managers and between managers and their subordinates. Team work is highly valued; managers are expected to set an example by committing time and resources to the development of their staff; refusal of a request should be accompanied by an explanation not an apology; access to superiors should not be restricted solely to the respective line manager.

While managerial hierarchies and structures are recognized, these were not viewed as barriers to a two-way flow of communication. Respondents rejected the proposition that subordinates' ideas and requests are valid only if transmitted through formal communication channels. The Polish managers were most emphatic in their rejection and the Romanians least so (with the difference statistically significant), reflecting possibly a contrast between Polish individualism and the autocratic style of Romanian managers. The proposition that 'ideas generated by informal groupings of managers may be ignored because such groupings are not considered legitimate' was rejected by all groups of managers in varying degrees. It was rejected most emphatically by Hungarian, Polish, Romanian and Slovenian managers and least so by Croat managers (the difference being statistically significant). A further proposition that 'managers should not introduce innovatory working practices unless formally approved by senior management' once again found general disagreement, most strongly among the Czechs and least so among the Croat managers.

In general, albeit with national variations of degree, there was a recognition of the role played by both formal and informal relationships in organizations. Formal structures and hierarchies are recognized but so too are informal mechanisms of interaction.

The respondents presented a general picture of support for ethical behaviour. Respondents found unofficial private use of a company's resources as basically unacceptable; it was considered acceptable to question a decision made by senior management on ethical grounds; operating within the law was regarded as not sufficient in itself and managers were expected to concern themselves with ethical issues.

Two propositions, however, elicited more varied responses. The proposition that 'loyalty to one's company should always take precedence over personal integrity' was most strongly accepted by Estonian managers, least so by Czech and Hungarian managers (with the differences statistically significant). A further proposition that 'undisclosed gifts to third parties are acceptable if they are necessary to secure an important contract' was most emphatically rejected by the Estonian managers and the least so by Croat and Polish managers (the differences again being statistically significant). The differences in the responses may indicate differing degrees of identification between individuals and their organizations, although all groups placed loyalty to the company before personal integrity. The responses relating to undisclosed gifts, although reflecting a general disapproval, display differences of degree which may derive from the general cultural background (for example, the influence of Lutheranism in Estonia).

Overall the managers recognized the significance of ethical behaviour in their responses, generally supporting ethical conduct by managers. The responses to the implementation of such behaviour are, as may be expected, more varied, recognizing that ethical behaviour concerns not only individuals but organizations. The proposition relating to undisclosed gifts also raises questions as to what is considered acceptable in different cultures.

Minor themes

The responses to statements exploring the issue of informal contacts are a development of aspects of the earlier themes of strategy and structure and colleagues and subordinates. Respondents were asked to comment on propositions relating to promotions within the company and to new business. The proposition that 'promotions within a company are often influenced by informal contacts' was strongly supported by Croat, Czech, Hungarian and Slovenian managers, with Polish managers tending to disagree with the proposition. The Polish response may indicate a wider dissemination and acceptance of formal systems in Poland, as mentioned earlier.

The proposition that 'most new business is the result of some informal contact rather than of cold-calling' was most emphatically rejected by the Polish respondents and least so by Czech, Estonian and Hungarian managers (with the differences statistically significant). Polish managers are thus in general more explicit than managers from the other countries surveyed in their rejection of the influence of informal factors both within and outside the organization, although the rejection is a question of degree rather than of absolutes.

There was strong agreement with the proposition that 'higher education and intelligence are important in enabling managers to see things clearly and to make rational decisions'. It has already been noted that managers viewed the development of staff as an important managerial activity. However, perceptions of company training sessions varied. The proposition that 'the main benefit of company training sessions is the opportunity they offer for getting to know people in other parts of the organization' was most emphatically rejected by the Estonian managers, with Croat, Hungarian and Romanian managers expressing least objection to the proposition. This possibly reflects a relatively greater significance of personal contacts and networking in countries such as Croatia, Hungary and Romania.

There was considerable variation in responses to propositions on the relationship between work and home/leisure. The proposition that 'managers owe it to themselves and their families to strike a sensible balance between the demands of work and home' was accepted by all national groups. However, Estonian and Polish managers were most emphatic in their support for the proposition with the Hungarians least so (the difference was statistically significant). The proposition that 'management work is fun! Discussions of the work/leisure distinction are not really meaningful' was generally rejected. Estonian managers rejected the proposition most strongly and Romanians least so (with the difference statistically significant).

Clearly the relationship between work and leisure is of considerable interest to managers. However, the responses reflected a varied range of views on the topic by national groups of managers, indicating differing perceptions of the relationship between work and leisure and possibly differing interpretations of the concepts of work, leisure and fun. For example, as mentioned in chapter 6, in practice Romanians draw a clear line between home and work.

National comparisons: Poland and the Czech Republic

The data were also analysed on the basis of two-country comparisons. Two-country comparisons highlight the similarities and differences between pairs of countries. An early analysis of part of the data contrasted managers' attitudes to change in the Czech Republic and Poland (Dytrt *et al.*, 1996). As in the overall survey there was considerable agreement in the way managers from the two countries view managerial work. However, a number of statistically significant differences between the two groups of managers also emerged. Compared with Polish managers Czech managers took a short-term rather than a long-term view (for instance, with regard to management work and business relationships). In contrast, Polish managers appeared to attach greater significance to formal structures and approaches than Czech managers. In general Polish managers, unlike their Czech counterparts, indicated a preference for formal systems rather than personal contacts.

The data indicated a number of clear differences between the managers from the two countries, for which a number of possible explanations come to mind. Firstly the two countries have undergone different historical experiences under communism. In general Poland was more open and flexible and provided greater scope for entrepreneurship than Czechoslovakia. The Catholic Church was a significant factor in creating these conditions. The degree of openness was also reflected in differences in the school and university systems. Poland's relative openness can be contrasted with the strongly controlled and closed system prevailing in Czechoslovakia, especially after the demise of the reforms of the Prague Spring of 1968. Compared to Poland Czechoslovakia experienced greater central command, adhered more closely to the Soviet model of central planning and was in general more tightly integrated in the Soviet bloc.

Further distinctive features were the greater exposure to and experience of contacts with western companies which many Polish managers had had since the 1980s. Moreover, there is a marked tendency to individualism in Polish culture, contrasting with a more collective approach in Czech society.

Secondly, there have also been differences in developments since 1989. The pace of transformation has been more rapid in Poland than in Czechoslovakia/the Czech Republic where the process of change has been subject to a higher degree of overall management by the government.

The Slovenian manager: the 'average' CEE manager?

The data analysis also indicated that Slovenian managers took in general a 'middle' view on the questions asked. The overall analysis brought to light 196 statistically significant differences (at the 5 per cent level) between countries for the total 86 statements, and 64 statistically significant differences for the 37 statements identified for further evaluation as mentioned earier in this chapter. In both instances the responses of the Slovenian managers accounted for the smallest number of statistically significant differences (7 and 3 respectively).

Starting with the three significant differences from the key 37 responses, these related to the following statements:

- Management and leadership are coterminous.
- Meeting short-term financial targets is the main criteria (*sic*) for promotion.
- Ideas generated by informal groupings of managers may be ignored because such groupings are not considered legitimate.

All national groups except the Croatian managers disagreed with the first two statements, with Hungarian, Polish and Romanian managers also disagreeing with the Croatian managers regarding the third statement.

The responses given by Slovenian managers to further statements relating to issues of management and decision-making, short-term motivation, and innovation and risk-taking elicited a similar pattern, with all national groups disagreeing significantly with Croatian managers in two instances and the same groups of managers as in the previous paragraph disagreeing significantly with Croatian managers in the third instance.

The data analysis revealed only one significant difference between Slovenian managers and another national group, apart from the Croatian managers. The statement in question was:

- Too much importance should not be attached to the notion of organizational structure: at the end of the day companies are made up of people who have to work with each other.

The response of the Slovenian managers was significantly different from that of their Polish counterparts who disagreed quite strongly with the statement, while the Slovenian managers were inclined to agree with the statement. The Polish response reflects the previously mentioned tendency of Polish managers to accept formal systems and procedures.

Overall, however, the Slovenian managers tended to give responses which did not differ significantly from those of their counterparts in the other countries surveyed (Croatia apart). On the vast majority of issues Slovenian managers reflected the majority view. An illustration of this is the response to the statement 'Management work is essentially about "fire-fighting" and removing "road blocks"'. The Slovenian response was very much a 'middle' one, reflecting possibly the degree of transition from a view of management based on short-term decisions and actions to one more concerned with longer-term and strategic issues. The extent of change in Slovenia has been less than in the other countries surveyed because Slovenia was already more advanced at the beginning of the transition because of the the country's experience of workers' self-management in the former Yugoslav Federation. Furthermore, the pace of transformation since 1990 has been in comparison to many of the other countries of CEE relatively gradual.

Croatian management

The responses from the Croatian managers elicited the highest number of statistically significant differences from the other national groups in the survey. Croatian managers tend to be generally more emphatic in their acceptance or rejection of particular propositions. This intensity of response may indicate a degree of frustration experienced by Croatian managers. Croatia had high economic and political aspirations as an independent state as a consequence of the collapse of Yugoslavia. These aspirations were frustrated by the conflict with Serbia and involvement in the Bosnian tragedy. War conditions thus held back political and economic progress, although the process of restructuring was intensified following the cessation of hostilities.

Eastern management/Western management

It is not surprising that the process of system change from command to market economy laid bare the weaknesses and deficiencies in knowledge and skills of individuals working in managerial and commercial positions within companies. The former system stressed specialist knowledge and skills, particularly of a technical nature, as enterprises were largely production units fulfilling the targets set by central planners, and the economic activities of enterprises were coordinated and controlled to a large degree by the ruling Communist Party. The operational activities of managers were therefore largely concerned with the practical implementation of enterprise plans – ensuring that necessary raw material inputs were obtained, that plant and equipment functioned effectively, or were repaired, bending the rules to meet (and exceed) the targets.

In general, managers in Central and Eastern Europe under the former system were well educated (the majority were graduates) and many held doctorates. How individuals became and evolved as managers was an integral part of the overall system of higher education which was dominated by the official ideology and the ruling Communist Party's socio-economic goals. Attainment of managerial positions, especially above middle management level, was in general dependent more on party affiliation and personal contacts than on professional competence itself, although the latter was not totally discounted. Managers were expected to demonstrate a certain level of technical competence (for example, as engineers). However, they often lacked strategic and general management skills. This was understandable to the extent that enterprises had only limited involvement in the planning process and general management functions were typically exercised by a combination of enterprise management, Communist Party officials and trade union representatives. Enterprises lacked the autonomy of companies in market economies and thus required different kinds of skills. The stress on technical expertise and implementation was reflected in the overall production-focused orientation of Central and East European managers. This orientation became a marked handicap after 1989, as companies needed to become more responsive to markets and the obsolete or obsolescent level of technology of many companies in the region became a serious handicap to future development.

A number of factors had influenced the development and career progression of managers under the communist regimes. Firstly there was a need to ensure the dissemination of the official ideology. The higher one rose within the enterprise hierarchy, the greater the significance of political affiliation became. Secondly, though deriving from this, political as well as social criteria were considered more important than purely economic criteria. A manager was more likely to be replaced for not 'towing the party line' than for being incompetent. In many cases incompetence resulted in being 'kicked upstairs'!

The main lines of the Soviet model of management comprised the following elements: (a) university degree (b) allocation to an enterprise and (c) party affiliation. In general, university education preceded permanent employment in an enterprise. There were, however, also opportunities for non-graduate practising managers to obtain academic qualifications by part-time study. The relative weighting attached to the elements of the model varied between countries and at different points in time but in general political affiliation predominated over competence, the higher one climbed up the managerial hierarchy (often to the detriment of performance).

The functioning of the system also resulted in a number of distortions. Although the level and availability of general university education were on the whole comparable and (in some cases) superior to higher education in Western Europe, the vagaries of the allocation systems led to bizarre placements of graduates (e.g. shipbuilders in pharmaceutical enterprises [Edwards and Lawrence, 1994]). Management development was also available but its development and effectiveness generally appeared somewhat limited when contrasted with the situation in the USA and Western Europe.

According to Granick (1975) East Germany and Romania had been in the forefront of managerial training in communist Central and Eastern Europe and the Romanian government had established a Management Development Centre in 1967. A Management Development Centre was established in Hungary in the 1970s. Interestingly, because of their greater openness to market forces, the former Yugoslav republics, with their emphasis on workers' self-management, did not begin setting up similar centres until the 1980s, when the Brdo Management School was established by the Slovenian Chamber of Commerce in 1986 (Warner, 1990), although business-related undergraduate courses were initiated in the late 1950s (Svetličič and Čibron, 1996).

The collapse of the communist regimes made necessary a complete overhaul of management education. Marxist economics was discredited and managers in the region clearly lacked the foundation of market-economy knowledge and skills enjoyed by Western managers. The overhaul of the system has been strongly influenced by American practice and the Anglo-Saxon model, although the Romance and Nordic models have also made an input through collaboration between universities, for example, supported by the EU's Tempus Programme. The overhaul has also been influenced by national traditions preceding the communist take-over of power. For example, the Hungarian university system was traditionally patterned on the German (Prussian) Model. The current situation is thus often a patchwork of former Soviet, pre-communist and imported practices.

A fundamental issue of this overhaul has concerned the meaning of management and the implicit meanings attached to the vocabulary of management. This semantic factor has varied from country to country. The following examples may serve as illustrations of this problematic. In Romania the word 'manager' is used to refer to the managing director or chief executive officer in a company, i.e. to the top manager. In Poland, as far as the word 'manager' and 'management' are concerned, 'there is no term in Polish which carries the connotations we expect' and words used to describe persons in managerial positions carry specific connotations of commanding and governing (Jankowicz, 1994).

This problem with meaning can be attributed to two main factors: the pre-communist and communist experiences of the countries in the region. East Germany and the Czech provinces apart, the countries of the region were largely agricultural prior to 1945; the industrial base was accordingly weak and a managerial class was little more than embryonic. The industrialization of the countries of the region under communist leadership followed the Soviet model which promoted bureaucratic rather than managerial-entrepreneurial modes of behaviour. The content and meaning of the work carried out by individuals in managerial positions consequently differed in significant ways.

Models of management

Each model of management has its own distinctive and distinguishing characteristics (Edwards and Lee, 1999). The former Soviet model fostered production-oriented specialization within the overall context of the official ideology, although technical specialism could in many respects be a way of lessening the political dimension. The Anglo-Saxon model is characterized by a stress on generalism allied to entrepreneurialism and the drive for profit. In the United Kingdom the model has been personified in the 'gifted amateur' who, irrespective of background, education or training, is capable of achieving business success. In contrast the Romance model cherishes intellectual elitism and that part of the educational system concerned with developing managers is seen as an incubator of cerebral Cartesian 'high flyers'. Whilst similarly stressing the importance of academic foundations and according substantial significance to high levels of qualification, the Nordic model has traditionally seen Technik (in particular as expressed in product engineering and manufacture) as the core of management.

Having highlighted the key aspects which distinguish the respective models from one another, can any common threads be identified? First, all the models – except traditionally the British version of the Anglo-Saxon model – attach great importance to academic development and training, and even the United Kingdom has changed considerably in this respect in recent years. Moreover, a common currency has evolved with the increasing dissemination of MBA programmes across Europe, irrespective of the locally dominant model. Second, and this applies to MBA programmes, the content and form of management courses remains strongly focused by the dominant local paradigm, albeit influenced to a degree by other models. Third, management development is increasingly providing portable qualifications both reflecting and encouraging management mobility. For example in the UK, the traditional model of internal upward mobility within one organization is yielding to greater mobility between organizations as managers can now provide evidence of universally accepted qualifications rather than just years of experience. There is also evidence of increasing mobility between organizations in CEE as managers gain wider experience and internationally recognized qualifications.

Even within the framework of particular models individual European countries have developed a distinctive managerial cadre (Lawrence and Edwards, 2000). This distinctiveness is reflected in each particular version of capitalism 'which is politically, socially and culturally embedded' (Zeleny 1993:46). How relevant is this to the situation and development of managers in Central and Eastern Europe?

First, the management cadres of individual countries derive from the general experience of economic and industrial development as well as from the particular system of education in each country. This experience is not consistent across the region. In this respect, compared to other former command economies of the region, the Czech Republic has a long-standing tradition of industrial development predating the communist period.

Second, management attitudes, behaviours and practices are embedded in deep-rooted social values and attitudes. In Britain it has been the gifted amateur (and gentleman) while in the USA it is the entrepreneur. Such stereotypes are significant in revealing widespread expectations of what a manager should be.

Third, imports are attractive but also problematical. Not all practices admired abroad are necessarily appropriate nor will they fit culturally with local practices. Existing cultural traditions need not only to be recognized but also built upon. This is likely to maintain diversity.

Under such circumstances the development of management in CEE will be influenced both conceptually and in practice by a number of factors:

- The Anglo-American model will continue to predominate because of general widespread American influence and the international currency of the MBA as a management qualification.
- Notwithstanding the predominance of the Anglo-American model, national differences in the way various models of management are implemented will persist.
- National variations in management will be conducive to better managerial practice, as managers in each country will be more closely attuned to broader social and cultural attitudes and values.
- Individual national cultures may in fact be better aligned with different models of management.

For example, national cultures characterized by a strong degree of individualism (Hofstede 1980) may be considered appropriate locations for the Anglo-American model. Such a situation may be considered to apply in Hungary, Poland and Slovenia. In more collectivist cultures such as the Czech Republic which also has a long-standing tradition of industrial development, the Nordic model with its stress on Technik may be more appropriate. On the other hand, the Romance model of management might be considered viable in, for example, Romania with its historial links to the Latin world and French culture and a more recent experience of industrialization. Such a culture-based approach is in line with Machkova's (1998) notion of zones of cultural affinities ('zones d'affinités culturelles') although not following Machkova's proposed classification which is specifically related to marketing policies.

The content and process of management development and change are also strongly influenced by the overall process of political, economic and social change in individual countries. One decade after the collapse of communism in CEE it was already evident that the former command economies were not progressing in a homogeneous manner and fast and slow developers could be relatively easily identified. Change is often most successful if built on a sound foundation of traditions and shared points of reference which in their turn are secured by the process of change (d'Iribarne, 1989:263–66). Continuity and change in this context go hand in hand, interacting with and reinforcing each other. In some countries, however, this relationship has not been mutually beneficial. Existing practices have held back and distorted the process of transformation. It is therefore likely that the development of managers in some of the countries will display for some time to come considerable differences from the western models of management.

References

Dytrt, Z., Edwards, V. and Witek-Hajduk, M. (1996) 'Managers' Attitudes to Change: The Czech Republic and Poland', in Edwards, V. (ed.), Proceedings of the CREEB Third Annual Conference, Chalfont St Giles: CREEB, pp. 332–36.

d'Iribarne, P. (1989) *La logique de l'honneur, Gestion des entreprises et traditions nationales*, Paris: Editions du Seuil.

Edwards, V. and Lawrence, P. (1994) *Management Change in East Germany*, London and New York: Routledge.

Edwards, V. and Lee, G. L. (1999) 'Models of Management Formation: Implications for Central and Eastern Europe', *Journal for East European Management Studies*, 4, 4, pp. 292–305.

Granick, D. (1975) *Enterprise Guidance in Eastern Europe, A Comparison of Four Socialist Economies*, Princeton UP.

Hofstede, G. (1980) *Culture's Consequences*, London: Sage, 1980.

Jankowicz, A. (1994) 'Parcels from Abroad: The Transfer of Meaning to Eastern Europe', *Journal of European Business Education*, 3(2), pp. 1–19.

Kiezun, W. (1991) *Management in Socialist Countries: USSR and Central Europe*, Berlin: De Gruyter.

Lawrence, P. (1998) *Issues in European Business*, Basingstoke and London: Macmillan.

Lawrence, P. and Edwards, V. (2000) *Management in Western Europe*, Basingstoke and London: Macmillan.

Machkova, H. (1998) 'Pratiques et politiques de marketing en Europe de l'Est', *revue française de gestion*, 117(1), pp. 107–115.

Svetličič M. and Čibron A. (1996) 'Management Education in a Country in Transition: The Case of Slovenia', in Amdam R. (ed.), *Management Education and Competitiveness*, London and New York: Routledge, pp. 111–30.

Warner, M. (1990) 'Management Versus Self-Management in Yugoslavia', *Journal of General Management*, vol. 16(2) Winter, pp. 20–38.

Zeleny, M. (1993) 'Reforms in Czechoslovakia: Traditions or Cosmopolitanism?', in Maruyama, M. (ed.), *Management Reform in Eastern and Central Europe*, Aldershot: Dartmouth, pp. 45–64.

Index

Alpina (company) 119–20
American management influence
  Poland 41
  Russia 45, 51–2
Anglo-American model of management
  143
Anglo-Saxon model of management 142
autarky see self-sufficiency of enterprises

Balcerowicz (finance minister) 38
Basic Organizations of Associated Labour
  (BOAL) 117, 118
Bata management system 65
Bosnia-Hercegovina 124–5
Brdo Management School, Slovenia 141
Bulgaria
  after communism 94–6
  background 90
  collectivization of agriculture 93
  corporate restructuring 97–8
  foreign direct investment 96
  industrialization 93
  managers' role 94, 98–100
  privatization 97
  and Russia 90–92
  tradition of hermitism 92
  under communist rule 91–4

Canada, economic dependence 109–10
Catholic Church, role in Poland 32
Ceausescu, Nicolae 13, 77–8
central planning
  consequences 8
  disappearance 11
COMECON 3–4, 67, 77, 86
  Bulgaria's role 93, 95, 96
  Hungary's role 18, 20, 25

command economy 3, 129
communication channels 135
communism 128
  collapse 131
  in Hungary 16–17, 22
Communist Party
  in Czechoslovakia 63–4
  influence 2, 3
  Nomenklatura 37, 68, 74
  in Poland 35, 36
  in Russia 48
companies, under socialist system 4–5
corporate governance system, Estonia
  113
corruption 131
Council for Mutual Economic Assistance
  (CMEA or COMECON) see
  COMECON
criminal activities 131
Croatia 124, 125
  managers' attitudes 139
Czech Republic
  background 61–2
  foreign direct investment 68
  managers' role 65–6
  market economy development 68–
  70
  national characteristics 64–5
  national identity 62–4
  Poland comparison 137–8
  privatization 67–8
  under socialism 66–7
Czechoslovakia, Communist Party 63–4

demand-constrained economies 3
departmental hierarchies, under socialist
  system 12

directive management model, Hungary
    16, 17–18

Eastern/Western management
    comparisons   140–42
economic performance, under command
    economy   129
enterprise directors, Russia   46–7
enterprises, under socialist system   4–5
Estonia
    1995 Business Code   113
    background   103–106
    corporate governance system   113–
        14
    external trade   107–108
    foreign direct investment   109,
        112–13
    free trade agreements   113
    Germanic influence   105
    industrial profile   106
    language features   110
    management style   110–12
    Nordic links   110
    open economy   112–13
    openness   110
    privatization   106–107
    sub-contracting   108–109
ethical behaviour standards   135–6
European Bank for Reconstruction and
    Development (EBRD)   50
European Union
    free trade agreement with Estonia
        113
    Hungary membership proposal   15

Fordism
    in Czechoslovakia   65
    in Russia   45
foreign competition   129
foreign direct investment (FDI)   129
    Bulgaria   96
    Czech Republic   68
    Estonia   109, 112–13
    Romania   80
    Russia   49–50
    Slovenia   119

Galati steel complex   87
German Treuhand privatization model
    107
gifts, undislosed   136
Gorbachev (Soviet President)   43, 47

guided market model, Hungary   16,
    19–20, 21

Hansabank   113
Hungary
    1956 uprising   18–19
    background   15
    directive management model   16,
        17–18
    enterprise autonomy   20, 21, 28
    guided market model   16, 19–20, 21
    Management Development Centre
        141
    New Economic Mechanism   21–3
    Oil Shock 1973 effects   20
    organizational diversity   29
    transition to market economy   25–9
    under communism   16–17
    university system   141
    wages and salaries   23, 26

integrity, personal   135

job security   12
joint ventures   130
    in Poland   35, 36

Kádár, János   18
Klaus, Vaclav   67
Kolektor (company)   120

Law on Cooperatives, Russia   47
Law on Ownership Transformation,
    Slovenia   121
Law on Privatization, Russia   51
Law on State Enterprises, Russia   47
Liuhto, Kari, management study
    110–12
loyalty (to company)   135

Macedonia   124
management of change   133
    in Russia   58–9
management cultures
    attitude survey   132–3
    development in CEE   143–4
    evolution   131
Management Development Centre
    Hungary   141
    Romania   141
management and employee buyouts,
    Slovenia   121

management models *see* models of
management
managers
 career paths 22
 Croatian attitudes 139
 motivation influences 7
 new roles 12, 21–2, 130
 performance 134–5
 political allegiance 22
 proactive role 27–8
 role under communism 128–9
 role under socialist system 5–7, 36–7
 Russian characteristics 50–51, 53,
 54–7
 Slovenian attitudes 138–9
 training 141
 work/leisure balance 137
 see also top managers
models of management
 Anglo-American 143
 Anglo-Saxon 142
 Nordic 142
 Romance 143
 Russia 140–41
 Soviet 14, 140–41, 142
monopolies, under socialist system 3
motivation influences 7

nationalization process 2–3
New Economic Mechanism, Hungary
 21–3
Nomenklatura 37, 68, 74
Nordic model of management 142

Official Romanian Culture 82
organizational structure 134
 Russia 57–8

plan fulfilment, under socialist system 9
Poland
 agriculture private ownership 34
 American management influence 41
 background 31–2
 and Catholic Church 32
 cultural values 32–6
 Czech Republic comparison 137–8
 manager-worker relations 41
 managers' role 36–7, 40, 41
 privatization opposition 38
 resistance to change 38–9
 Second World War consequences 34
 'Shock Therapy' experience 38

worker organization 35
world trade links 35–6
political leverage 5, 56
Prague Spring 64, 66, 67, 93
private ownership of property 2
privatization
 effects 129
 pace 130
 western comparisons 107

Ratowski (prime minister) 37
resource-constrained economies 3
Romance model of management 143
Romania
 background 77–8
 business culture 82
 change barriers 85–8
 foreign direct investment 80
 GDP level 80
 industrialization 79
 Management Development Centre
 141
 managers' role 83–5
 national identity 80–82
 Official Romanian Culture 82
 privatization 80, 87
 shock therapy regime 78–9
 under communist rule 78, 79
Russia
 American management influence 45,
 51–2
 background 43–4
 characteristics of managers 54–7
 company indebtedness 51
 corruption risks 57
 demise of Communist Party 48
 enterprise directors 46–7
 enterprise structure changes 50
 entrepreneurism growth 56–7
 foreign direct investment 49–50
 Law on Privatization 51
 management learning 58–9
 managers' role 50–51
 market economy establishment 47–9
 organizational management 57–8
 post World War I development 44–6
 price liberalization policy 48–9
 privatization 49
 shock therapy reform package 48, 49
 superpower role 44, 45
 top managers' role 51–2
 typology of managers 53

self-sufficiency of enterprises   9
Slovak Republic, background   61–2
Slovakia
  background   71–2
  corporativist system   74
  management changes   73–4
  privatization   73
Slovenia
  Austrian influence   119
  background   118–19
  Brdo Management School   141
  companies after 1990   119–20
  enterprise restructuring   122
  foreign direct investment (FDI)   119
  GDP   124
  Law on Ownership Transformation
    121
  management and employee buyouts
    121
  managers' role   120–21, 123–4,
    138–9
  privatization   121–2
  quality management   122
  top managers' role   122, 123–4
socialist system   1–4
  changes   10–13
  collapse   8
  diversity   13–14
  effect of external influences   9
  enterprises function   4–5
  living conditions   10
  managers' role   5–7, 36–7
  Yugoslav model   116–18
soft budget constraints   5
Solidarity (trade union)   31, 33, 35
Soviet Union, model of management   14,
    140–41, 142
staff development   136
state property   2, 3
statistics, manipulation   8

Supreme Economic Council (SEC),
    Hungary   17
survey of management attitudes   132–3

Tallinn stock exchange   113
Taylorism
  in Czechoslovakia   65
  in Russia   45
top managers
  bonus allocations   23–4
  discretion limitations   24–5
  in Hungary   27
  in Poland   37, 39–40
  in Russia   51–2
  in Slovenia   122, 123–4
  strategic role   133, 134
Treuhand privatization model   107

'Velvet Divorce'   61, 70–71

wages and salaries, Hungary   23
work/leisure balance   137
workforce, under socialist system   6,
    128

Yeltsin, Boris (Soviet President)   43, 48
Yugoslav Federation   115–16
  collapse   118
Yugoslavia
  background   115–16
  decentralization   116–17
  GNP   118
  guest workers   117
  model of socialism   116–18
  other republics   124–5
  self-management system   117–18,
    120–21
  social ownership   116

Zenica steel works   125